The Foundation Center's

Guide to Proposal Writing

Revised Edition

Jane C. Geever

Patricia McNeill

THE
FOUNDATION
CENTER

Library of Congress Cataloging-in-Publication Data

Geever, Jane C.
   The Foundation Center's guide to proposal writing / Jane C.
Geever, Patricia McNeill. — Rev. ed.
      p.   cm.
   Includes bibliographical references.
   ISBN 0-87954-703-0
   1. Proposal writing for grants—United States—Handbooks, manuals,
etc.   I. McNeill, Patricia, 1941–   II. Foundation Center.
III. Title.
HG177.5.U6G44   1997
658.15'224—dc21   97-6283
                                                              CIP

Contents

Preface

For many years, grantseekers using Foundation Center libraries and publications frequently asked us for help beyond the research into potential funders for their work. They wanted assistance in writing the proposal and advice on the proper way to submit it, given the widely differing policies and preferences among foundations and corporate grantmakers. To respond to this demand, in 1993 we commissioned Jane C. Geever and Patricia McNeill of the firm, J. C. Geever, Inc., to write this book for us, based on their many years of combined fundraising experience and on interviews with a great variety of grantmakers. This revised 1997 edition includes grantmaker responses to a new series of interview questions and excerpts from a new group of proposals to illustrate the text.

We hope this guide to proposal writing proves useful to all of you who are seeking grants, and we would welcome your comments and reactions to it.

We wish to thank the following grantmakers who participated in the interviews for their time and the valuable insights they provided:

F. Worth Hobbs, President
Alcoa Foundation
Pittsburgh, PA

Cynthia E. Merritt, Associate
    Secretary
Carnegie Corporation of New York
New York, NY

Bruce L. Newman, Executive
    Director
The Chicago Community Trust
Chicago, IL

Susan N. Lajoie, Associate Director
The Cleveland Foundation
Cleveland, OH

J. Andrew Lark, Co-Trustee
The Frances L. & Edwin L.
    Cummings Memorial Fund
New York, NY

Christine Park, Director
Dayton Hudson Foundation
Minneapolis, MN

Jane Quinn, Program Director
DeWitt Wallace-Reader's Digest
    Fund, Inc.
New York, NY

Reatha Clark King, President and
    Executive Director
General Mills Foundation
Minneapolis, MN

Ilene Mack, Senior Program Officer
William Randolph Hearst
    Foundation
New York, NY

Hunter W. Corbin, Vice President
The Hyde and Watson Foundation
Chatham Township, NJ

Eugene R. Wilson, President, Youth
    Development
Ewing Marion Kauffman
    Foundation
Kansas City, MO

John E. Marshall III, President
The Kresge Foundation
Troy, MI

Deborah Wallace, Executive
    Director
Levi Strauss Foundation
San Francisco, CA

John W. Cook, President
The Henry Luce Foundation, Inc.
New York, NY

Alicia Philipp, Executive Director
Metropolitan Atlanta Community
    Foundation, Inc.
Atlanta, GA

Julie L. Rogers, President
Eugene and Agnes E. Meyer
    Foundation
Washington, DC

John L. Mason, President
Monsanto Fund
St. Louis, MO

Marijane R. Lundt, Program Officer
The Prudential Foundation
Newark, NJ

Hildy Simmons, Managing Director
J. P. Morgan & Co., Incorporated
New York, NY

Alberta Arthurs, Director of Arts
  and Humanities
The Rockefeller Foundation
New York, NY

Joyce M. Bove, Vice President,
  Programs and Projects
The New York Community Trust
New York, NY

We also wish to thank the nonprofit organizations who graciously permitted us to use excerpts from their proposals to illustrate the text.

Brooklyn Children's Museum
Brooklyn, NY
Bobye G. List, Executive Director

Contra Costa College
San Pablo, CA
Frank Hernandez, Assistant Dean
  of Instructional Technology

Center for Families and Children
Cleveland, OH
Richard L. Jones, President and
  Chief Executive Officer

D.C. Hunger Action
Washington, DC
Colleen Fee, Executive Director

East Side House Settlement
Bronx, NY
John A. Sanchez, Executive Director

Center for Responsive Politics
Washington, D.C.
Ellen S. Miller, Executive Director

Edenwald-Gun Hill Neighborhood
  Center, Inc.
Bronx, NY
Jessie W. Collins, Executive Director

Children's Television Workshop
New York, NY
Ellen S. Buchwalter, Director of
  Development

Georgia Center for Children, Inc.
Atlanta, GA
La Vann P. Weaver, Executive
  Director

CLEARPOOL
New York, NY
Peter B. Rose, President

The HOPE Program
Brooklyn, NY
Barbara Edwards Delsman,
  Executive Director

Cleveland Institute of Art
Cleveland, OH
Robert A. Mayer, President

Kenmare High School
Jersey City, NJ
Sister Agnes Fox, Administrator

Mind-Builders Family Services
    Center
Bronx, NY
Camille Giraud Akeju, Executive
    Director

Phillis Wheatley Association
Cleveland, OH
Joyce R. Daniels, Executive Director

Planned Parenthood of Westchester
    & Rockland, Inc.
Hawthorne, NY
Francine Stein, Executive Director

Project Reach Youth
Brooklyn, NY
Janet Kelley, Executive Director

Project Renewal
New York, NY
Edward I. Geffner, Executive
    Director

Recruiting New Teachers, Inc.
Belmont, MA
David Haselkorn, President

Summit Area YMCA
Summit, NJ
Timothy Weidman, Executive
    Director

Teach for America
New York, NY
Julian Johnson, Director of
    Development

WomenVenture
St. Paul, MN
Kay Gudmestad, President

Youth Development Institute
New York, NY
Michele Cahill, Vice President

YWCA of Plainfield/North
    Plainfield
Plainfield, NJ
Jacquelyn M. Glock, Executive
    Director

From the Authors

Proposal writing is essential to the fundraising process, but it can be intimidating for the novice. There is nothing worse than staring at a blank piece of paper or computer screen with the sinking feeling that so much is riding on the prose you must create. Yet, if you follow the step-by-step process described in this book, you can create a proposal with a minimum of anxiety.

Take the steps one at a time. You will be successful in writing exciting and compelling proposals, proposals that will capture the interest of foundations and corporations, proposals that will generate grant support for your nonprofit organization.

In preparing this book, we interviewed a cross section of foundation and corporate representatives to find out their current thoughts on what should go into a proposal. While this material reinforces the steps we describe for writing a proposal, it also presents some notable insights into how grantmakers do their work, the challenges facing funders today, and how they are responding. These insights are a distinguishing feature of this book: they show the reality of the fundraising process from the funder's side of the proposal.

The 21 funding representatives interviewed include a geographic mix of local and national foundations, four community foundations, and seven company foundations. Some of the funders represented have been in existence for many years. Others are fairly new. All are large enough to have at least one person on staff, and some employ many people.

While the grantmakers interviewed reflect a relatively broad spectrum, it is important to remember that there are more than 38,500 foundations in the United States. The majority of these have no staff and in fact are so small that the few local grants they award each year can be handled by trustees, lawyers, or family members. Therefore, the comments made here do not necessarily apply to all funders, but they do provide an indication of how some of the larger funders operate and how they evaluate the proposals they receive.

A series of questions was designed for the interview sessions in order to elicit views not only on proposal writing but also on the entire funding process. Interviews were conducted via the telephone, following a questionnaire format. Questions were posed as to desired proposal contents, layout, length, and presentation. Funders were asked how proposals captured and kept their attention, what the characteristics of a successful proposal are, and what red flags are raised when they read proposals. They were also asked to discuss follow-up strategies once an agency receives a grant and whether, and how, to resubmit a rejected proposal. They were asked to describe trends they perceived in the funding climate of the 1990s.

Information and quotes gleaned from these interviews are used throughout the text. Appendix A, "What the Funders Have to Say," reflects the substance of the interviews. Here, the reader can find specific questions asked of each grantmaking representative with some of their responses. The goal in presenting this information is distinctly not to help the reader learn about particular funders but rather to provide a more general sense of grantmakers' perspectives on proposal writing. The funders interviewed have spoken frankly.

They have all granted permission to the Foundation Center to use their quotes.

Acknowledgments

We would like to express appreciation to the staff of J. C. Geever, Inc., particularly to Cheryl Austin who helped prepare the manuscript, and to Margaret Morth and Cheryl Loe of the Foundation Center who saw this guide through production.

Introduction

If you are reading this book, you have probably already decided that foundations should be part of your fundraising strategy. You should be aware that, together, foundations and corporations provide only about 11 to 12 percent of private gift support to nonprofit institutions. Their support, however, can be extremely important in augmenting other forms of support, in permitting major new initiatives, or simply in promoting the mission of your agency.

Foundation giving has increased dramatically in recent years. During the decade of the 1980s, more than 3,000 foundations with assets over $1 million or annual grants budgets of $100,000 or more were created. The assets of the foundation field tripled during the decade both because of these new players and because of the rise in the value of the assets held by existing foundations. By 1995, foundations held combined assets of over $236 billion and made grants totaling more than $12 billion.

Unfortunately, competition for these grant dollars has also increased. Many nonprofits are being created to deal with new or heightened social needs. Cutbacks in government funding for nonprofit services and activities have meant that many groups that previously relied primarily on government funds are now turning to private sources to support their work.

In comparison with the figures for foundation giving, according to the American Association of Fund-Raising Counsel (AAFRC) Trust for Philanthropy, giving by individuals was almost $125 billion in 1995, 11 times that of foundations. There is money out there. What you need to attract it to your agency is a comprehensive fundraising strategy that includes a variety of sources and approaches. This book focuses on how to create proposals to win foundation and corporate support.

You will want to tell your story clearly, keeping the needs of those you are approaching in mind. You need to recognize the potential for partnership with those you are approaching.

The Proposal Is Part of a Process

The subject of this book is proposal writing. But the proposal does not stand alone. It must be part of a process of planning and of research on, outreach to, and cultivation of, potential foundation and corporate donors.

This process is grounded in the conviction that a partnership should develop between the nonprofit and the donor. When you spend a great deal of your time seeking money, it is hard to remember that it can also be difficult to give money away. In fact, the dollars contributed by a foundation or corporation have no value until they are attached to solid programs in the nonprofit sector.

This truly *is* an ideal partnership. The nonprofits have the ideas and the capacity to solve problems, but no dollars with which to implement them. The foundations and corporations have the financial resources but not the other resources needed to create programs. Bring the two together effectively, and the result is a dynamic collaboration. Frequently, the donor is transformed into a stakeholder in the grantee organization, becoming deeply interested and involved in what transpires.

"We view ourselves as a partner with the nonprofit," says Eugene Wilson of the Ewing Marion Kauffman Foundation.

John Mason of the Monsanto Fund adds that the grantmaker and grantseeker both have to invest time and energy in the relationship to make it work. "Get the message out: grantseekers need to recognize that grantmakers invest in people, not organizations. The grantmaker has got to understand the people behind the application. Nonprofits are not inanimate objects. Grantseekers frequently don't see the need to invest the time to build a relationship."

Other funders also speak of investing in people. In the opinion of Julie Rogers of the Eugene and Agnes E. Meyer Foundation, "Giving is one human to another." And Reatha Clark King of the General Mills Foundation draws attention to the interconnection among the ideas of relationship, partnership, and trust. She refers to these concepts as "heavy-duty words."

You need to follow a step-by-step process in the search for private dollars. It takes time and persistence to succeed. After you have written a proposal, it could take a year or more to obtain the funds needed to carry it out. And even a perfectly written proposal submitted to the right prospect might be rejected for any number of reasons.

Raising funds is an investment in the future. Your aim should be to build a network of foundation and corporate funders, many of which give small gifts on a fairly steady basis, and a few of which give large, periodic grants. By doggedly pursuing the various steps of the process, each year you can retain most of your regular supporters and strike a balance with the comings and goings of larger donors. The distinctions between support for basic, ongoing operations and special projects are discussed elsewhere in this book. For now, keep in mind that corporate givers and small family foundations tend to be better prospects for annual support than the larger, national foundations.

The recommended process is not a formula to be rigidly adhered to. It is a suggested approach that can be adapted to fit the needs of any nonprofit and the peculiarities of each situation. Fundraising is an art, not a science. You must bring your own creativity to it and remain flexible.

An example might help. It is recommended that you attempt to speak with the potential funder prior to submitting your proposal.

The purpose of your call is to test your hypothesis gleaned from your research about the potential match between your nonprofit organization and the funder. Board member assistance, if you are fortunate enough to have such contacts, ordinarily would not come into play until a much later stage. But what do you do if a board member indicates that his law partner is chairman of the board of a foundation you plan to approach? He offers to submit the proposal directly to his partner. You could refuse the offer and plod through the next steps, or you could be flexible in this instance, recognizing that your agency's likelihood of being funded by this foundation might have just risen dramatically. Don't be afraid to take the risk.

Recognizing the importance of the process to the success of your agency's quest for funds, let's take a look at each step.

Step One: Setting Funding Priorities

In the planning phase, you need to map out all of your agency's priorities, whether or not you will seek foundation or corporate grants for them. Ideally these priorities are determined in an annual planning session. The result of the meeting should be a solid consensus on the funding priorities of your organization for the coming year. Before seeking significant private sector support, you need to decide which of your organization's funding priorities will translate into good proposals. These plans or projects are then developed into funding proposals, and they form the basis of your foundation and corporate donor research.

Step Two: Drafting the Basic or "Master" Proposal

You should have at least a rough draft of your proposal in hand before you proceed, so that you can be really clear about what you'll be asking funders to support. In order to develop a "master" proposal, you will need to assemble detailed background information on the project, select the proposal writer, and write the actual components of the document, including the executive summary, statement of need, project description, budget, and organizational information.

Step Three: Packaging the Proposal

At this juncture you have laid the groundwork for your application. You have selected the projects that will further the goals of your organization. You have written the master proposal, usually a "special project" proposal, or a variation, such as one for a capital campaign or endowment fund.

Before you can actually put the document together and get it ready to go out the door, you will need to tailor your "master" proposal to the specific funder's needs. When you have taken that step, you will need to add a cover letter and, where appropriate, an appendix, paying careful attention to the components of the package and how they are put together.

Step Four: Researching Potential Funders

You are now ready to identify those sources that are most likely to support your proposal. You will use various criteria for developing your list, including the funders' geographic focus and their demonstrated interest in the type of project for which you are seeking funds. This research process will enable you to prepare different finished proposal packages based on the guidelines of specific funders.

Step Five: Contacting and Cultivating Potential Funders

This step saves you unnecessary or untimely submissions. Taking the time to speak with a funder about your organization and your planned proposal submission sets the tone for a potentially supportive future relationship, *if* they show even a glimmer of interest in your project. This step includes judicious use of phone communication, face-to-face meetings, board contacts, and written updates and progress reports. Each form of cultivation is extremely important and has its own place in the fundraising process. Your goal in undertaking this cultivation is to build a relationship with the potential donor. Persistent cultivation keeps your agency's name in front of the foundation or corporation. By helping the funder learn more about your group and its programs, you make it easier for them to come to a positive response on your proposal—or, failing that, to work with you in the future.

Step Six: Responding to the Result

No matter what the decision from the foundation or corporate donor, you must assume responsibility for taking the next step. If the response is positive, good follow-up is critical to turning a mere grant into a true partnership.

Unfortunately, even after you have followed all of the steps in the process, statistically the odds are that you will learn via the mail or a phone call that your request was denied. Follow-up is important here, too, either to find out if you might try again at another time or with another proposal or to learn how to improve your chances of getting your proposal funded by others.

1

Getting Started: Establishing a Presence and Setting Funding Priorities

Every nonprofit organization needs to raise money. That is a given. Yet some nonprofits believe that their group must look special or be doing something unique before they are in a position to approach foundations and corporate grantmakers for financial support. This assumption is mistaken. If your organization is meeting a valid need, you are more than likely ready to seek foundation or corporate support.

But three elements should already be in place. First, your agency should have a written mission statement. Second, your organization should have completed the process of officially acquiring nonprofit status, or you need to have identified an appropriate fiscal agent to receive the funds on your behalf. Finally, you should have credible program or service achievements or plans in support of your mission.

Mission Statement

When your agency was created, the founders had a vision of what the organization would accomplish. The mission statement is the written summary of that vision. It is the global statement from which all of your nonprofit's programs and services flow. Such a statement enables you to convey the excitement of the purpose of your nonprofit, especially to a potential funder who has not previously heard of your work. Of course, for you to procure a grant, the foundation or corporation must agree that the needs being addressed are important ones.

Acquiring Nonprofit Status

The agency should be incorporated in the state in which you do business. In most states this means that you create bylaws and have a board of directors. It is easy to create a board by asking your close friends and family members to serve. A more effective board, though, will consist of individuals who care about the cause and are willing to work to help your organization achieve its goals. They will attend board meetings, using their best decision-making skills to build for success. They will actively serve on committees. They will support your agency financially and help to raise funds on its behalf. Potential funders will look for this kind of board involvement.

In the process of establishing your nonprofit agency, you will need to obtain a designation from the federal Internal Revenue Service that allows your organization to receive tax-deductible gifts. This designation is known as 501(c)(3) status. A lawyer normally handles this filing for you, and it can take up to 18 months to obtain this designation. Legal counsel can be expensive. However, some lawyers are willing to provide free help or assistance at minimal cost to organizations seeking 501(c)(3) status from the IRS.

Once your nonprofit has gone through the filing process, you can accept tax-deductible gifts. If you do not have 501(c)(3) status and are not planning to file for it in the near future, you can still raise funds. You will need to find another nonprofit with the appropriate IRS designation willing to act as a fiscal agent for grants received by your agency. How does this work? Primary contact will be between your organization and the funder. The second agency, however, agrees to be responsible for handling the funds and providing financial reports. The funder will require a formal written statement from the agency serving as fiscal agent. Usually the fiscal agent will charge your organization a fee for this service.

Credible Programs

Potential funders will want to know about programs already in operation. They will invest in your agency's future based on your past achievements. You will use the proposal to inform the funder of your accomplishments, which should also be demonstrable if an on-site visit occurs.

If your organization is brand new or the idea you are proposing is unproven, the course you plan to take must be clear and unambiguous. Your plan must be achievable and exciting. The expertise of those involved must be relevant. Factors such as these must take the place of a track record when one does not yet exist. Funders are often willing to take a risk on a new idea, but be certain that you can document the importance of the idea and the strength of the plan.

Like people, foundations have different levels of tolerance for risk. Some will invest in an unknown organization because the proposed project looks particularly innovative. Most, however, want assurance that their money is going to an agency with strong leaders who have proven themselves capable of implementing the project described in the proposal.

What really makes the difference to the potential funder is that your nonprofit organization has a sense of direction and is implementing, or has concrete plans to implement, programs that matter in our society. You have to be able to visualize exciting programs and to articulate them via your proposal. Once you've got these three elements in place, you're ready to raise money from foundations and corporations!

Setting Funding Priorities

Once your organization has established a presence, the first step of the proposal process is determining the priorities of your organization.

Only after you do that can you select the right project or goals to turn into a proposal.

Your Priorities

There is one rule in this process: You must start with your organization's needs and then seek funders that will want to help with them. Don't start with a foundation's priorities and try to craft a project to fit them. Chasing the grant dollar makes little sense from the perspectives of fundraising, program design, or agency development.

When you develop a program tailored to suit a donor, you end up with a project that is critically flawed. First, in all likelihood the project will be funded only partially by the grant you receive. Your organization is faced with the dilemma of how to fund the rest of it. Further, it will likely be hard to manage the project as part of your total program without distorting your other activities. Scarce staff time and scarcer operating funds might have to be diverted from the priorities you have already established. At worst, the project might conflict with your mission statement.

Start with a Planning Session

A planning session is an excellent way to identify the priorities for which you will seek foundation grants and to obtain agencywide consensus on them. Key board members, volunteers, and critical staff, if your agency has staff, should come together for a several-hour discussion. Such a meeting will normally occur when the budget for the coming fiscal year is being developed. In any case, it cannot be undertaken until the overall plan and priorities for your organization are established.

The agenda for the planning session is simple. With your organization's needs and program directions clearly established, determine which programs, needs, or activities can be developed in proposal form for submission to potential funders.

Apply Fundability Criteria

Before moving ahead with the design of project proposals, test them against a few key criteria:

1. The money cannot be needed too quickly. It takes time for funders to make a decision about awarding a grant. If the foundation or corporate grantmaker does not know your agency, a cultivation period will probably be necessary.

   A new program can take several years to be fully funded, unless specific donors have already shown an interest in it. If your new program needs to begin immediately, foundation and corporate donors might not be logical sources to pursue. You should begin with other funding, from individuals, churches, or civic groups, from earned income, or from your own operating budget, or else you should delay the start-up until funding is secured from a foundation or corporate grantmaker.

   A project that is already in operation and has received foundation and corporate support stands a better chance of attracting additional funders within a few months of application. Given your track record, a new funder will find it easy to determine that your nonprofit can deliver results.

2. Specific projects tend to be of greater interest to most foundation and corporate funders than are general operating requests. This fundraising fact of life can be very frustrating for nonprofits that need dollars to keep their doors open and their basic programs and services intact. There is no doubt, though, that it is easier for the foundation or corporate funder to make a grant when the trustees will be able to see precisely where the money is going, and the success of their investment can be more readily assessed.

   Keep in mind the concerns of the foundation and corporate funders about this question when you are considering how to develop your proposals for them. You may have to interpret the work of your organization according to its specific functions. For example, one nonprofit agency uses volunteers to advocate in the courts on behalf of children in the foster care system. Its goal is to bring about permanent solutions to the children's situations. When this agency first secured grants from foundations and corporations, it did so for general support of its program. Finding their supporters reluctant to continue providing general support once the program was launched, the staff began to write proposals for specific aspects of the agency's work, such as volunteer recruitment, volunteer training, and advocacy, thus making it easier for donors to continue to fund ongoing, core activities.

Some foundations do give general operating support. You will use the print and electronic directories, annual reports, the foundations' own 990-PFs, and other resources described elsewhere in this book to target those that are true candidates for operating and annual support requests if you find that your funding priorities cannot be packaged into projects. Alternatively, your general operating dollars *might* have to come from nonfoundation sources.

3. Support from individual donors and government agencies might be better sources for some of the priorities you are seeking to fund. Moreover, having a diverse base of funding support is beneficial to the financial well-being of your nonprofit agency. Foundation and corporation support usually should be augmented by support from individuals in the form of personal gifts raised via face-to-face solicitation, special events, and direct mail and/or by earned income in the form of fees or dues.

You know the priorities of your organization. You have determined which ones should be developed for submission to foundations and corporations in the form of a proposal. You are now ready to move on to the proposal-writing step.

2

Developing the Master Proposal: Preparation, Tips on Writing, Overview of Components

One advantage of preparing the master proposal before you approach any funders is that all of the details will have been worked out. You will have the answers to just about any question posed to you about this project.

Another advantage is that usually you will need to customize only the cover letter, to reflect the connection between your agency and that particular funder or to take note of their specific program priorities. Few funders require a separate application form or special format.

Gathering Background Information

The first thing you will need to do in writing the master proposal is to gather the documentation for it. You will require background documentation in three areas: concept, program, and expenses.

If all of this information is not readily available to you, determine who will help you gather each type of information. If you are part of a small nonprofit with no staff, a knowledgeable board member will be the logical choice. If you are in a larger agency, there should be program and financial support staff who can help you. Once you know with whom to talk, identify the questions to ask.

This data-gathering process makes the actual writing much easier. And by involving other stakeholders in the process, it also helps key people within your agency seriously consider the project's value to the organization.

Concept

It is important that you have a good sense of how the project fits into the philosophy and mission of your agency. The need that the proposal is addressing must also be documented. These concepts must be well-articulated in the proposal. Funders want to know that a project reinforces the overall direction of an organization, and they might need to be convinced that the case for the project is compelling. You should collect background data on your organization and on the need to be addressed so that your arguments are well-documented.

Program

Here is a checklist of the program information you require:

- the nature of the project and how it will be conducted;
- the timetable for the project;
- the anticipated outcomes and how best to evaluate the results; and
- staffing needs, including deployment of existing staff and new hires.

Expenses

You will not be able to pin down all of the expenses associated with the project until the program details and timing have been worked out. Thus, the main financial data gathering takes place after the narrative part of the master proposal has been written. However, at this stage you do need to sketch out the broad outlines of the budget to be sure that the costs are in reasonable proportion to the outcomes you anticipate. If it appears that the costs will be prohibitive, even with a foundation grant, you should then scale back your plans or adjust them to remove the least cost-effective expenditures.

Deciding Who Will Write the Proposal

While gathering data, you can make the decision about who will actually write the document. You might decide to ask someone else to draft it for you. This is a tough decision. If the obvious staff member you identify to write the first draft will have to put aside some other major task, it might not be cost-effective for the agency, and you might consider whether someone else on staff is a skilled writer or a willing learner and could be freed up from routine assignments.

If you lack a staff member with the skills and time to take on the task, a volunteer or board member might be an excellent alternative. You will need to identify someone who knows the agency and writes well. You will spend substantial time with this person, helping to describe the kind of document you want. In the long run, this can be time well spent, because you now have identified a willing and skilled volunteer proposal writer.

If you have found your writer on staff or among your volunteer ranks, you are all set. The information for the proposal has been gathered, and work can commence. Should you fail to find someone this way, then an outsider will be needed. Bear in mind, before you choose this option, that the most successful proposals are often "home grown," even if they aren't perfect. A too-slick proposal obviously written by an outsider can be a real turnoff to funders.

On the other hand, while someone inside your agency will always know your organization better than a consultant, an outsider can bring objectivity to the process and may write more easily, especially with the data gathering already complete. Once the decision is made to use a consultant, you will need to make a list of prospective consultants, interview the leading candidates, check references, and make your selection.

You and the consultant will develop a contract that adequately reflects the proposed relationship. This document should include:

- details on the tasks to be performed by the consultant;
- the date when the contract becomes effective and the date of its expiration;
- a cancellation clause that can be exercised by either party within a specific number of days' notice, usually not less than 30 or more than 90 days;
- a statement that the agency owns the resulting proposal;
- information on the fee that the consultant will be paid and when it is to be paid (perhaps tying it to delivery of the product or completion of specified tasks);
- details on reimbursement of out-of-pocket expenses or on an expense advance on which the consultant may draw; and
- a provision for the contract to be signed both by the consultant and by an officer of the nonprofit.

If possible, your nonprofit organization should use legal counsel in developing the contract. At a minimum an attorney should review the document to see that the agency's interests are protected. Seek out *pro bono* legal assistance. Do not consider oral agreements to be binding on either side. Put everything in writing.

Tips on Writing the Proposal

Regardless of who writes the proposal, grant requests are unique documents. They are unlike any other kind of writing assignment. Here are some tips for the proposal writer:

For many grantseekers, the proposal is the *only* opportunity to communicate with a foundation or corporate donor.

The written document is the one thing that remains with a funder after all the meetings and telephone calls have taken place. It must be self-explanatory. It must reflect the agency's overall image. Your proposal will educate the funder about your project and agency. It will motivate the potential funder to make a gift.

You do need to put as much care into preparing your proposal as you have put into designing the project and as you are planning to put into operating it. You have spent a fair amount of time determining priorities for raising funds and gathering the appropriate information for the proposal. The information you have collected should be thoroughly woven into an integrated whole that dramatically depicts your agency's project for the funder.

There are some basic rules that apply to all writing and a few that are peculiar to proposals for foundations and corporations.

Get Your Thoughts Sorted Out

A proposal must deliver critical ideas quickly and easily. Your writing must be clear if you want others to understand your project and become excited by it. It will be hard to accomplish this if you have not clarified your thoughts in advance.

This means identifying the central point of your proposal. All of your subsequent points should flow easily from it. Once you have clearly thought through the broad concepts of the proposal, you are ready to prepare an outline.

Outline What You Want to Say

You understand the need for the program. You have already gathered the facts about how it will unfold, if funded. You have identified the benchmarks of success and the financial requirements. With this information in hand, outline what should be said and in what order. If you take the time to create this outline, the process of writing will be much easier, and the resulting proposal will be stronger. Rushing to write a document without an outline only leads to frustration, confusion, and a poorly articulated proposal.

Avoid Jargon

Jargon confuses the reader and hampers the reviewer's ability to comprehend your meaning. It impedes your style. It may be viewed as pretentious. With so much at stake in writing a proposal, it makes sense to avoid words (and acronyms) that are not generally known and to select words for their precision.

Be Compelling, but Don't Overstate Your Case

People give to people. While your proposal has to present the facts, it must let the human element shine through. Personify the issue. Tell your story with examples. Illuminate your vision so that the funder can share it with you. Don't be afraid to humanize the materials once the facts are in place. But never assume that your writing is so compelling that programmatic details are unnecessary. A number of the grantmakers interviewed for this guide indicated a preference for real-life examples to enhance the text of a proposal. In the words of Alberta Arthurs of the Rockefeller Foundation, "I think proposals today are getting a bit too cut-and-dried. They need a little rounding. A bit of anecdotal information is helpful if it achieves that rounding."

Try to be realistic in presenting your case. Take care that in your enthusiasm you do not overstate the need, the projected outcomes, or the basic facts about your organization.

It is dangerous to promise more than you can deliver. The proposal reviewer is sure to raise questions, and the result could be damaged credibility with the funder. Worse, if the proposal is funded, and the results do not live up to the exaggerated expectations, future support is jeopardized.

Keep It Simple

In the old days, fundraisers believed that the longer the document and the more detail it had, the better it was and the more money could be requested. Today, foundation and corporate funders look for concisely presented ideas. Eliminate wordiness. Simply present the key thoughts.

Keep It Generic

As you progress through the fundraising process, you may well approach a number of different potential funders with the same or a similar proposal. Thus, it makes sense to develop a master proposal that, with certain customizing touches, can be submitted to a number of sources. This does not mean that you must have access to fancy word-processing equipment. A clean photocopy of the basic proposal, accompanied by a typewritten cover letter, is acceptable to most funders.

In many areas of the country, groups of foundations have agreed to adopt a common application form. It makes sense to inquire as to whether one exists in your geographic area and whether the funder you are applying to accepts proposals in this form. The very same careful research that goes into identifying appropriate funders pertains to contacting those that accept common application forms. Examples of common application forms can be found at the Foundation Center's World Wide Web site at http://fdncenter.org.

COMPONENTS OF A PROPOSAL

Executive Summary:	umbrella statement of your case and summary of the entire proposal	1 page

Statement of Need:	why this project is necessary	2 pages

Project Description:	nuts and bolts of how the project will be implemented	3 pages

Budget:	financial description of the project plus explanatory notes	1 page

Organization Information:	history and governing structure of the nonprofit; its primary activities, its audiences, its services	1 page

Conclusion:	summary of the proposal's main points	2 paragraphs

Revise and Edit

Once you have completed the proposal, put it away temporarily. Then in a day or two, reread it with detachment and objectivity, if possible. Look for the logic of your arguments. Are there any holes? Move on to analyzing word choices and examining the grammar. Finally, give the document to someone else to read. Select someone with well-honed communication skills, who can point out areas that remain unclear and raise unanswered questions. Ask for a critical review of the case and of the narrative flow. This last step will be most helpful in closing any gaps, in eliminating jargon, and in heightening the overall impact of the document.

A well-crafted document should result from all these hours of gathering, thinking and sifting, writing and rewriting. Carol Robinson, executive director of the Isaac H. Tuttle Fund, provides us with an ideal to strive for: "To me a proposal is a story. You speak to the reader and tell the reader a story, something you want him/her to visualize, hear, feel. It should have dimension, shape and rhythm and, yes, it should 'sing.' Words are another way to draw a picture, to carve, to create music, to blow glass, to weave, to make porcelain." (private letter, December 30, 1985)

The following chapters include many examples to assist you in better understanding the points being made. A number of these are excerpts from actual proposals and are reprinted with permission from the issuing agency. Please note that to keep the design of the book simple, we did not reproduce these examples in their original formats.

No two proposals are precisely the same in their execution, and no single proposal is absolutely perfect. In fact, some of the examples presented here have flaws. These examples are used to underscore a specific point, but together they illustrate the more general one that flexibility on the part of the proposal writer is essential. In a winning proposal, often the nature of the issues being addressed overrides rules about format.

A full sample proposal appears in Appendix B.

3

Developing the
Master Proposal:
The Executive Summary

This first page of the proposal is the most important section of the entire document. Here you will provide the reader with a snapshot of what is to follow. Specifically, it summarizes all of the key information and is a sales document designed to convince the reader that this project should be considered for support. Be certain to include:

Problem—a brief statement of the problem or need your agency has recognized and is prepared to address (one or two paragraphs);

Solution—a short description of the project, including what will take place and how many people will benefit from the program, how and where it will operate, for how long, and who will staff it (one or two paragraphs);

Funding requirements—an explanation of the amount of grant money required for the project and what your plans are for funding it in the future (one paragraph); and

Organization and its expertise—a brief statement of the name, history, purpose, and activities of your agency and its capacity to carry out this proposal (one paragraph).

How will the executive summary be used? First, in the initial review of your request, it will enable the funder to determine that the proposal is within their guidelines. Then it is often forwarded to other staff or board members to assist in their general review of the request. If you don't provide a summary, someone at the funder's office may well do it for you and emphasize the wrong points.

Here's a tip: It is easier to write the executive summary last. You will have your arguments and key points well in mind. It will be concise. Ideally, the summary should be no longer than one page or 300 words.

Here is an example of an executive summary, taken from a proposal submitted by Project Renewal to the Frances L. & Edwin L. Cummings Memorial Fund. This summary immediately identifies the financial request. It provides an excellent synopsis of the problem and the proposed solution.

Project Renewal

Proposal: MedVan Social Worker

Project Renewal requests from the Francis L. & Edwin L. Cummings Memorial Fund a grant of $25,000 to support the addition of a Social Worker to our Mobile Medical Outreach Clinic—or *MedVan*, as it is known on the streets of New York.

Launched in 1986, MedVan was the nation's first mobile medical clinic to serve homeless people, providing primary care and referrals to thousands of indigent New Yorkers on the street, and in the shelters, soup kitchens, and drop-in centers where they congregate.

Two critical factors make it urgently necessary to break more new ground by adding a Social Worker to MedVan's professional team: first, MedVan's patients are displaying ever more complex suites of medical problems, often requiring multiple visits and long term care to arrive at a complete diagnosis and treatment—a situation that has severely stretched the capacity of MedVan's medical professionals; second, though MedVan patients often qualify for medical entitlements and other public services, they frequently need help in obtaining them—a need that MedVan's medical team has valiantly tried to satisfy, while also trying to meet an ever more demanding patient load.

Adding a Social Worker to MedVan will solve these problems by:

- Helping significantly more patients to obtain entitlements and other services;
- Tracking patients through referrals, which will encourage them to take full advantage of available services;
- Freeing the MedVan team to treat more patients;
- Resulting in more repeat patients, which will enable the MedVan team to perform more complete diagnoses and treatment.

The ultimate benefit of this initiative will be improved health among MedVan's homeless patients. This is an absolutely essential step in the process of helping homeless people to rehabilitate themselves—which is Project Renewal's mission.

Another example comes from a proposal written for the Frances L. & Edwin L. Cummings Memorial Fund by the HOPE Program.

Proposal Summary

For over a decade, The HOPE Program has intervened in the lives of homeless and unemployed men and women who indicate that they can achieve self-sufficiency if given appropriate training and support. Founded in 1984 at a time when most homeless programs provided only emergency assistance, HOPE began to address the underlying causes of homelessness with a comprehensive strategy of support and education to promote economic independence and participation in mainstream society.

At the heart of HOPE's program is an intensive 14-week *Job-Readiness Training* program which offers on-going counseling and work internships, with educational and computer instruction at our new *Literacy Center,* and follow-up activities for graduates to help them succeed in the work world. The HOPE method yields remarkable results: 67% of our students secure employment or enroll in continuing education programs within six months of their graduation and 68% of our graduates are still employed after two years.

We are now seeking a $20,000 grant from the Frances L. & Edwin L. Cummings Memorial Fund to support our efforts to replicate our program in underserved communities in New York City. Specifically, given HOPE's growing reputation for providing an exceptionally effective and innovative model of intervention for the homeless and unemployed, we are now receiving a large number of replication inquiries from social service agencies both within and outside of New York City. One replication project was launched successfully just last year at Genesis Homes in East New York. Funding would support the New York efforts of our recently established Replication and Technical Assistance Team (R&TA), which is devoted to training other agencies in our methods, as we continue to evaluate and improve our own program model.

Neither example contains every element of the ideal executive summary, but both persuasively present the case for reading further.

4

Developing the Master Proposal: The Statement of Need

If the funder reads beyond the executive summary, you have success-fully piqued his or her interest. Your next task is to build on this initial interest in your project by enabling the funder to understand the problem that the project will remedy.

The statement of need will enable the reader to learn more about the issues. It presents the facts and evidence that support the need for the project and establishes that your nonprofit understands the prob-lems and therefore can reasonably address them. The information used to support the case can come from authorities in the field, as well as from your agency's own experience.

You want the need section to be succinct, yet persuasive. Like a good debater, you must assemble all the arguments and then present them in a logical sequence that will readily convince the reader of their importance. As you marshal your arguments, consider the following six points:

First, decide which facts or statistics best support the project. Be sure the data you present are accurate. There are few things more embarrassing than to have the funder tell you that your information is out of date or incorrect. Information that is too generic or broad will not help you develop a winning argument for your project. Information that does not relate to your organization or the project you are presenting will cause the funder to question the entire proposal. There should be a balance between the information presented and the scale of the program.

An example might be helpful here. Your nonprofit organization plans to initiate a program for battered women, for which you will seek support from foundations and corporations in your community. You have on hand impressive national statistics. You can also point to an increasing number of local women and their children seeking help. However, local data is limited. Given the scope of the project and the base of potential supporters, you should probably use the more limited local information only. It is far more relevant to the interest of funders close to home. If you were to seek support from more nationally oriented funders, then the broader information would be helpful, supplemented by details on local experience.

Second, give the reader hope. The picture you paint should not be so grim that the situation appears hopeless. The funder will wonder whether an investment in a solution will be worthwhile. Here's an example of a solid statement of need: "Breast cancer kills. But statistics prove that regular check-ups catch most breast cancer in the early stages, reducing the likelihood of death. Hence, a program to encourage preventive checkups will reduce the risk of death due to breast cancer." Avoid overstatement and overly emotional appeals.

Third, decide if you want to put your project forward as a model. This could expand the base of potential funders, but serving as a model works only for certain types of projects. Don't try to make this argument if it doesn't really fit. Funders may well expect your agency to follow through with a replication plan if you present your project as a model.

If the decision about a model is affirmative, you should document how the problem you are addressing occurs in other communities. Be sure to explain how your solution could be a solution for others as well.

Fourth, determine whether it is reasonable to portray the need as acute. You are asking the funder to pay more attention to your proposal because either the problem you address is worse than others or the solution you propose makes more sense than others. Here is an example of a balanced but weighty statement: "Drug abuse is a national problem. Each day, children all over the country die from drug overdose. In the South Bronx the problem is worse. More children die here than any place else. It is an epidemic. Hence, our drug prevention program is needed more in the South Bronx than in any other part of the city."

Fifth, decide whether you can demonstrate that your program addresses the need differently or better than other projects that preceded it. It is often difficult to describe the need for your project without being critical of the competition. But you must be careful not to do so. Being critical of other nonprofits will not be well received by the funder. It may cause the funder to look more carefully at your own project to see why you felt you had to build your case by demeaning others. The funder may have invested in these other projects or may begin to consider them, now that you have brought them to their attention.

If possible, you should make it clear that you are cognizant of, and on good terms with, others doing work in your field. Keep in mind that today's funders are very interested in collaboration. They may even ask why you are not collaborating with those you view as key competitors. So at the least you need to describe how your work complements, but does not duplicate, the work of others.

Sixth, avoid circular reasoning. In circular reasoning, you present the absence of your solution as the actual problem. Then your solution is offered as the way to solve the problem. For example, the circular reasoning for building a community swimming pool might go like this: "The problem is that we have no pool in our community. Building a pool will solve the problem." A more persuasive case would cite what a pool has meant to a neighboring community, permitting it to offer recreation, exercise, and physical therapy programs. The statement might refer to a survey that underscores the target audience's planned usage of the facility and conclude with the connection between the proposed usage and potential benefits to enhance life in the community.

The statement of need does not have to be long and involved. Short, concise information captures the reader's attention. This is the case in the following example from a proposal by the HOPE Program.

The Need for The HOPE Program

An estimated 90,000 people in New York City are homeless and unemployed. Among them are thousands of men and women who are potentially employable but have been sidetracked by any number of difficulties: problems with chemical dependency; physical, emotional, and/or family issues; loss of housing due to spousal abuse, fires, or eviction. Many wish to re-enter mainstream society but find the task insurmountable.

Even the most determined cannot negotiate their way out of a situation in which they have no resources: no home, no appropriate clothing, no carfare, no phone, no way to put together a resume. And even more debilitating than these practical obstacles is the profound loss of confidence and self-esteem which accompanies homelessness and unemployment. Specific and ongoing assistance is required in order for these traumatized individuals to develop the skills, confidence, and competence that will enable them to achieve and maintain economic self-sufficiency.

Studies have shown that on-the-job training by itself is expensive and relatively ineffective. A more comprehensive approach to self-sufficiency is needed, one that includes clinical assessment, counseling, behavioral modfication, and assistance with medical and emotional problems, to affect real and lasting change. Through all of HOPE's programs, students are helped to identify the underlying difficulties that brought them into their current situations and to develop practical strategies to return to mainstream society. With HOPE's innovative approach to training, work experience and counseling, the record shows that they *can* make the transition to employment and self-sufficiency.

The next example comes from a proposal to the Eugene and Agnes E. Meyer Foundation submitted by D.C. Hunger Action. Since this is a request from a local agency to a grantmaker based in the same geographic area, the need section relies appropriately on local data and information.

Purpose of Grant

Needs to be Addressed

People are hungry in Washington, D.C. In one of the wealthiest cities in the nation, in the richest country in the world, thousands of people go hungry every day. Roughly 30,000 people—nearly half of them young children—face chronic food shortages in the nation's capital.

The faces of hunger are many. They include senior citizens who must choose between paying for medicine and paying for food; people with AIDS whose specialized diets absorb much of their income; mothers who deny themselves food in order to conserve food for their children; and little kids who attack their school breakfast on Monday because it is the only thing they've eaten since Friday.

Hunger is especially prevalent among families with children. According to the findings of D.C. Hunger Action's Community Childhood Hunger Identification Project, approximately 24,500 out of 80,000 District children under 12—about one in four—are hungry or at risk of being hungry. About 11,000 children under age 12 in the District of Columbia are hungry, and an additional 13,500 are at risk of hunger. Hungry children live in households in which everyone suffers from hunger. At-risk children live in households in which some, but not all, family members feel the effects of food shortages.

Hunger is caused by insufficient economic, family, and community resources. Hungry families regularly run out of money to buy food. In conducting the CCHIP study, D.C. Hunger Action learned that sixty percent of the District's low-income households regularly run out of money to buy food. Nearly thirty percent of low-income parents surveyed stated that their children ate less than they should on an average of 36 occasions during the previous year because there was not enough money to buy food. About a quarter of respondents said that their children had to cut the size of their meals or skip meals altogether an average of 43 times during the previous year because the family had run out of money to buy food. One in eleven respondents admitted that their child sometimes went to bed without having had enough to eat because the family lacked money for food. Children in these households went to bed hungry an average of 36 nights in the previous year.

When the money runs out and their friends and family cannot provide relief, hungry families turn to public assistance programs. With more than fourteen programs making up the food assistance safety net, low-income people in need should be able to access nutritious food at every stage of their lives. In fact, poor outreach, cumbersome application procedures, poorly-trained personnel, low benefits, inadequate program funding, and stigma prevent many people from accessing the nutritious food they need. Even those who negotiate the application process and are awarded benefits find that these benefits are insufficient to prevent hunger: forty percent of those participating in the School Breakfast Program still experience hunger, as do over one-third of those receiving food stamps.

A final example is from a proposal submitted by Contra Costa College to the General Mills Foundation. Results of a preliminary survey conducted among the population to be served were presented as part of the need statement but are omitted here for the purpose of brevity.

Parent Education for School Involvement

Description of the Problem to be Addressed

The essence of the problem to be addressed by this proposed project is the disparity between Latinos' hopes and dreams for their children's success and the school's ability and willingness to address their children's needs, partially based on school staff's perception of Latino parents as uninterested and unable to participate in their children's educational process. It is this disparity between the parents' expectations of the schools and the schools' expectations of the parents which forms the core of this problem—a problem of both cultural dissonance and mutual misperception. In order to understand the severity of these issues, it is helpful to get a sense of the Richmond community and the West County School District, as well as to explore the disparity between school and parent expectations regarding appropriate and effective educational roles.

Located in West Contra Costa County, the City of Richmond is an economically-depressed area with approximately 40% of its population receiving some form of public assistance. Richmond has one of the highest employment rates in the San Francisco Bay Area. The residents of the community are predominantly members of minority groups with high percentages of South East Asian immigrants, African-Americans, and Latinos, both recently immigrated and long-time residents. As media coverage will validate, violence has become a daily threat in this community plagued by gang strife, poverty, under-education, and increasing racial tensions.

The enrollment of the West Contra Costa School District, formerly the Richmond Unified School District and the first district in California to go bankrupt, now exceeds 35,000 students. More than 65% of the student population are of minority ethnicity. 35–40% of the incoming freshmen will not graduate with a high school degree. The largest percentages of these non-graduates are Latinos. Standardized test scores for K-12 students are among the lowest in the county. Students from the district have a low college entrance rate, and, with the elimination of one class period from the high school and two from the junior high, it will be increasingly difficult for students to prepare for a college education. These statistics coupled with the ongoing financial difficulties of the district and the State promise a bleak future for youth, particularly students of color.

The parents, statistically speaking, are poor, uneducated, often unemployed or working in menial jobs. The local library's literacy project estimates that 40% of Richmond's urban dwellers are functionally illiterate. The children from these families need more evidence that they can achieve a better quality of life by staying in school and developing strong work skills.

As you can see from all three examples, the need statement begins the process whereby the organization builds its case and tells its story. This process continues in the next section of the proposal, which describes how the project will address the need.

5

Developing the
Master Proposal:
The Project Description

In this section, describe the nuts and bolts of the project in a way that gets the reader excited about it, while making a compelling case for the approach you have adopted. It is worth stating right up front that your plan is not written in stone. It might change based on feedback on your proposal and the experience you gain through implementation. It is not worth putting your organization in a defensive position in negotiating with grantmakers, and you certainly don't want to surprise a funder in the project's final report when you state that you changed your approach.

This section of your proposal should have four subsections: objectives, methods, staffing/administration, and evaluation. Together, objectives and methods dictate staffing and administrative requirements. They then become the focus of the evaluation to assess the results of the project. The four subsectors present an interlocking picture of the total project.

Objectives

Objectives are the measurable outcomes of the program. They help delineate your methods. Your objectives must be tangible, specific, concrete, measurable, and achievable in a specified time period. Grantseekers often confuse objectives with goals, which are conceptual and more abstract. For the purpose of illustration, here is the goal of a project with a subsidiary objective:

Goal: Our afterschool program will help children read better.

Objective: Our afterschool remedial education program will assist 50 children in improving their reading scores by one grade level as demonstrated on standardized reading tests administered after participating in the program for six months.

The goal in this case is abstract: improving reading, while the objective is much more specific. It is achievable in the short term (six months) and measurable (improving 50 children's reading scores by one grade level).

With competition for dollars so great, well-articulated objectives are increasingly critical to a proposal's success.

Using a different example, there are at least four types of objectives:

1. Behavioral—A human action is anticipated.
   Example: Fifty of the 70 children participating will learn to swim.

2. Performance—A specific time frame within which a behavior will occur, at an expected proficiency level, is expected.
   Example: Fifty of the 70 children will learn to swim within six months and will pass a basic swimming

proficiency test administered by a Red Cross–certified lifeguard.

3. Process—The manner in which something occurs is an end in itself.
   Example: We will document the teaching methods utilized, identifying those with the greatest success.

4. Product—A tangible item results.
   Example: A manual will be created to be used in teaching swimming to this age and proficiency group in the future.

In any given proposal, you will find yourself setting forth one or more of these types of objectives, depending on the nature of your project. Be certain to present the objectives very clearly. Make sure that they do not become lost in verbiage and that they stand out on the page. You might, for example, use numbers, bullets, or indentations to denote the objectives in the text. Above all, be realistic in setting objectives. Don't promise what you can't deliver. Remember, the funder will want to be told in the final report that the project actually accomplished these objectives.

The example that follows is from Contra Costa College. It is a brief statement of the proposed project's objectives, presented in two paragraphs.

Program Purpose

The purpose of this program is to educate Latino parents to become involved in their children's education by actively participating in school-based activities, establishing frequent communication with their children's teachers, establishing and maintaining a home environment fostering literacy, modeling literacy behaviors, and rewarding students for educational achievement.

Description of the Program

This proposed three-year program of parent education has a three-pronged emphasis: educating parents regarding the schools' expectations of them; establishing a formal and ongoing link between the teachers, parents, students, and the CCC Metas Program; and providing parents with homework-specific literacy training such that they will begin to feel comfortable helping their children (even if it is only the young students) with their homework.

Another example is from a proposal submitted to the DeWitt Wallace–Reader's Digest Fund by the Youth Development Initiative of the Fund for the City of New York. It is an example of a clear statement of objectives for a project.

YDI seeks an 18 month grant to carry out the first year and a half of planning activities for a subsequent three-year initiative to implement an adaptation of Beacons School-based Community Centers nationally in selected localities. This proposal envisions the entire project over four years, beginning in May, 1996. It includes identification of goals, a problem statement, a plan of action, a project assessment plan, a discussion of project institutionalization and costs for both the planning and implementation phases of the entire Beacons Adaptation Project.

The objectives of the Beacons Adaptation Project include the following:

- promoting affiliation with the vision of Beacons, especially by strengthening the presence and contribution of community-based youth serving organizations in schools;

- strengthening youth development programming in school settings, especially programs emphasizing educational enrichment and career development;

- increasing the presence of readiness factors in communities that are planning implementation of Beacon-like community schools;

- supporting leadership development for extended day services for youth by creating a peer technical assistance network which builds capacity in the community-based organization community including executive directors, youth workers and city leaders;

- increasing knowledge about key factors involved in successful implementation of youth services in school-based settings;

- supporting effective implementation of Beacon-like community schools across the country, with programming across the four key areas characterizing the Beacons model: youth development, parent involvement, school-community linkages, and building supportive neighborhoods for children and youth;

- increasing capacity for effective youth development services within school-community collaborations by identifying and providing support to local capacity-building organizations; and

- promoting institutionalization of Beacon-like community schools, especially through strategies for institutionalizing funding for community schools.

Methods

By means of the objectives, you have explained to the funder what will be achieved by the project. The methods section describes the specific activities that will take place to achieve the objectives. It might be helpful to divide our discussion of methods into the following: how, when, and why.

How: This is the detailed description of what will occur from the time the project begins until it is completed. Your methods should match the previously stated objectives. In our example about teaching 50 children to swim, appropriate methods would describe: 1) how the youngsters will be recruited, 2) how they will be taught to enhance their skills, and 3) how their swimming skills will be measured. There would be no reason to describe an extraneous activity like helping the parents learn to enjoy swimming with their children, because using swimming to bring the family together in wholesome exercise is not a stated objective of the project.

CLEARPOOL, in its proposal to the Frances L. & Edwin L. Cummings Memorial Fund, presents action steps so that they support specific objectives. An excerpt follows:

Dissemination Goals

Our first goal for 1995/96 is to complete the intensive planning and development for the start-up year at JBCFS and the development of our third school. Throughout the summer, we have collaborated with the JBCFS principal to interview prospective teachers and develop curriculum, governance and management systems. In addition, we began a new collaborative partnership with the Vocational Foundation, Inc., to provide employment training and job placement services to parents and siblings. Consistent with CLEARPOOL's philosophy, JBCFS will include a Family Center, Extended Day programs and residential programming at the Carmel campus. Our Core Planning Committee—comprised of the JBCFS's Principal, Assistant Principal, CLEARPOOL President and Vice President of Education, and the Project Director of Vocational Foundation Inc.—will direct and monitor the initial integration of our model's components throughout this crucial start-up phase.

Toward creating our third school, strategic planning meetings between CLEARPOOL and the District 10 Superintendent are underway, and as partners, we have applied to become a "New Vision School" through the second round of the Fund for New York City Public Education's reform effort. CLEARPOOL staff and the District Superintendent are actively negotiating with program service providers, hiring teacher-directors and program staff, overseeing preparation of the physical plant, and securing the necessary funding for the school, scheduled to open in the fall of 1996. In addition, we are developing a comprehensive proposal to be presented to the Chancellor's office for the planning and development of a CLEARPOOL "Demonstration School."

The second goal relating to dissemination is to provide critical teacher and staff training and professional development. The JBCFS teachers and program staff have already begun a series of retreats, trainings, and information sessions to learn and embrace CLEARPOOL's philosophies, methods and teaching practices. In August, Decatur-Clearpool and JBCFS staff participated in a three-day retreat at the Carmel campus to share knowledge and experience, and will convene again at Carmel in October to continue to develop joint curricula. The October weekend will also include training in instructional technology, and dialoging with other professionals to develop lesson plans and assess student progress. Throughout the course of the year, teachers and staff will participate in workshops led by experts in education, social service, and psychology, and have many other individual opportunities for professional development.

As we begin to realize our vision of replication by growing the network of CLEARPOOL educational sites, our third goal, building a state-of-the-art technology program, is critical to facilitating ongoing development of CLEARPOOL's model. Enhanced technology systems will facilitate continuity of curriculum at all sites, provide teachers with valuable tools for lesson planning and student assessments, and link each site to share vital information. This year, we plan to install local area networks at each site and a wide area network linking JBCFS, Decatur-Clearpool, the Carmel Campus, Gramercy Park administration, and Sponsors for Educational Opportunity's 31st Street Manhattan location. Day school teachers will be able to communicate with Extended Day teachers and Carmel teachers on individual student progress and on integrating day, afterschool and residential curricula. The network will facilitate cross-site communication and record keeping that is crucial for integrated education. Teachers will have access and contribute to "electronic portfolios" about each student, with complete quantitative and qualitative data. Networks will allow teachers and staff to share successful curriculum and program ideas, participate in open dialogues, pose questions and participate in collaborative decision making—via computer. Rather than having to meet in person, teachers and staff will log on to the network to pose a question about evaluations, curriculum development or "real life" applications of concepts, and receive expedient responses and information. This will free valuable time for teaching and program development.

Our fourth dissemination goal stems from our belief that no effort to replicate our model is appropriate without guaranteeing the continuing excellence and ongoing refinement of all the CLEARPOOL educational and service components. Recently, CLEARPOOL has made several changes in order to increase its capacity and improve the quality of its educational programs. First, we have expanded our collaboration with Sponsors for Educational Opportunity (SEO) to create a natural progression for students graduating from CLEARPOOL model schools in the eighth grade to the academic enrichment programs, mentoring and college and career preparation at SEO. CLEARPOOL will increasingly work with SEO on the planning and implementation of programs for children and families to ensure this continuity.

Think about how you can most readily construct a logical sequence from each objective to its relevant method. This can be accomplished in a number of ways, some relating simply to visual placement on the page.

One means of organizing this section is to write out each objective and to list beneath it the method(s) that will make the objective possible. It would look like this:

Objective: to recruit 70 children

Methods:

- Put up signs in the Y.
- Go to each school and address classes on the fun of swimming.
- Put ads in the local paper.
- Enclose a flyer about the program with the next mailer sent out to each family in the community.

The methods should match the magnitude of the objectives. Once you are sure that each objective has related methods that describe how the objective will be achieved, you should check that the emphasis given each method matches the importance of the related objective. In our swimming example, recruitment of 70 children is probably the least important objective; demonstrating that 50 of them can pass the Red Cross test is more critical. To match the magnitude of the objectives with appropriate detail about the project, more emphasis should be placed on the testing than on recruiting. (This refining and highlighting of information will enable the reader to understand the project and to have confidence in your agency.)

The methods should appear doable; otherwise, you lose credibility. For example, if the swimming course is to be taught by an Olympic swimmer who remains anonymous, the reader might question whether the organization can deliver what it has promised. However, if the Olympic star is identified by name and has already agreed to run the program, the reader will likely be convinced.

When: The methods section should present the order and timing for the tasks. It might make sense to provide a timetable so that the reader does not have to map out the sequencing on his own. The timetable could look like the one excerpted from a Children's Television Workshop project:

Lead Poisoning Project Timeline Draft

Month	Tasks
April	**Materials Development**
	Tape of blood test
	Video script treatment
	Identify/hire songwriter(s)
	Identify/hire music producer
	Determine video content
	Start decisions on brochure content
	Research
	Extended information-gathering
	Outreach
	Begin identifying conferences for presentations
May	**Materials Development**
	First draft of script
	Script for comments
	Brochure draft
	Research
	Testing of existing materials, as needed
	Testing of audio recording of video script

June	**Materials Development**
	Prepare "scratch" video for Research to test
	Send script of revised video to advisors for comments
	1st revision of brochure
	Circulate brochure copy to advisors for comments
	Research
	Test "scratch" video
	Research findings
July	**Materials Development**
	Final script revisions
	Video shoot, July 20–21
	Research
	Test video components, as needed
August	**Outreach**
	Draft distribution plan
September	**Materials Development**
	1st draft guide to go with video
	Feedback on guide
	Revise guide
	Video post-production
	Final draft brochure
	Audio script
	Guide and brochure to advisors
	Solicit & review manufacturing bids
October	**Materials Development**
	Print design
	Research
	Conduct audio research
	Conduct print research

Outreach

Finalize distribution plan
Conferences, ongoing

November **Materials Development**

Print/package design
Audio production
Finalize manufacturing contracts

Research

Continue research on audio and print
Research findings
Develop reply card copy and design

Outreach

Conferences, ongoing

Launch Event

Schedule and begin planning

December **Materials Development**

Audio final revise
Audio production
Print final copy revise
Print final design

Research

Final reply card copy and design

Another presentation of a solid work plan is from an East Side House Settlement proposal. It succinctly describes work to be undertaken over a three year grant period.

Calendar of Activity

The requested $20,000 in Pinkerton Foundation support during the next program year will allow us to:

- present one College Fair in the Fall of 1996, as previously described;
- collaborate with an additional college (either Bronx Community or Lehman College) to provide internship positions and mentoring partners, increasing the total number of internship positions available to 20;
- expand our offerings at the College Resource Center to meet the demands of our community outreach efforts; and
- evaluate the results of the first program year with the help of Miguel Matos from University of Connecticut.

With the requested $15,000 in Pinkerton Foundation support for 1997–1998 we will:

- continue all activities to date;
- add another collaborating college (Bronx Community or Lehman) that offers internships, increasing the total number of internship positions available to 25; train 8 additional student mentors from that participating college; increasing the mentoring program to 25 college-age mentors;
- increase outreach to 200 students and community residents at area high schools, including Cathedral High School; and
- evaluate the results of the program in its permanent configuration.

During the final year of The Pinkerton Foundation support, with the $10,000 requested, we will institutionalize the program as part of the East Side House core offerings, and:

- continue all activities to date;
- maintain 25 program interns;
- outreach to 200 students who attend workshops and use the College Resource Center;

> - train 13 mentors per year to maintain a core group of 25 college mentors; and
> - conduct a summative evaluation.

The timetable tells the reader "when" and provides another summary of the project that supports the rest of the methods section.

Why: You need to defend your chosen methods, especially if they are new or unorthodox. Why will the planned work lead to the outcomes you anticipate? You can answer this question in a number of ways including using examples of other projects that work and expert testimony.

The methods section enables the reader to visualize the implementation of the project. It should convince the reader that your agency knows what it is doing, thereby establishing credibility.

Staffing/Administration

In describing the methods, you will have mentioned staffing for the project. You now need to devote a few sentences to discussing the number of staff, their qualifications, and specific assignments. Details about individual staff members involved in the project can be included either as part of this section or in the appendix, depending on the length and importance of this information.

"Staffing" can refer to volunteers or to consultants, as well as to paid staff. Most proposal writers do not develop staffing sections for projects that are primarily volunteer-run. Describing tasks that volunteers will undertake, however, can be most helpful to the proposal reader. Such information underscores the value added by the volunteers and the cost-effectiveness of the project.

For a project with paid staff, be certain to describe which staff will work full time and which will work part time on the project. Identify staff already employed by your nonprofit and those to be recruited specifically for the project. How will you free up the time of an already fully deployed individual?

Salary and project costs are affected by the qualifications of the staff. Delineate the practical experience you require for key staff, as well as level of expertise and educational background. If an individual has already been selected to direct the program, summarize his or her credentials and include a brief biographical sketch in the appendix. A strong project director can help influence a grant decision.

Explain anything unusual about the proposed staffing for the project. It is better to include such information in the proposal narrative than to have the funder raise questions once the proposal review begins.

Three samples of staffing sections follow. The first is part of a proposal by D.C. Hunger Action. This example discusses collaborating organizations, paid staff, and volunteer support.

Other organizations participating and their roles

D.C. Hunger Action intends to collaborate with the Campaign to End Childhood Hunger and the Food Research and Action Center on the national level, the Fair Budget Coalition on the local level, and a variety of hunger and poverty-related organizations.

The Campaign to End Childhood Hunger and the Food Research and Action Center will provide D.C. Hunger Action with information and analysis on major hunger-related legislation. D.C. Hunger Action will then distribute this information to participants in the Fair Budget Coalition and other service providers, along with tips on how to educate policy makers about the impact of pending legislation on low-income people.

The Fair Budget Coalition will also help D.C. Hunger Action monitor local happenings. In working with that group, DCHA will take the lead on organizing and advocating around any legislation that impacts hunger.

The Fair Budget Coalition and local service providers will make up D.C. Hunger Action's database of advocates.

Staffing of the project

The food policy program is currently run by Colleen Fee, D.C. Hunger Action's executive director, and a volunteer, Panravee Vongjareonrat. Colleen has a master's degree in social work from Boston College, where she concentrated in community organizing, policy and planning. Before taking over D.C. Hunger

---

Action, Colleen worked as State Policy Associate at the Alliance for Young Families. There she organized member organizations to learn about state budget and administrative issues; trained them to advocate on behalf of the pregnant and parenting teens they represented; and provided them with policy memos, bulletins, and fact sheets.

Panravee graduated from Georgetown Law Center in May 1995. She first came to DCHA in May 1994 as part of a summer fellowship program. After observing Panaravee's work that summer, D.C. Hunger Action decided to hire her as a work study student for the 1994-95 academic year. Although she has graduated from law school, Panravee continues to remain involved with D.C. Hunger Action as a volunteer. She takes on individual clients' cases in disputes with the food stamp office, conducts research around policy issues, and writes fact sheets and newsletter articles.

As long as the policy program remains relatively limited in scope, Colleen will remain the project director, and Panravee will assist her on a volunteer basis. Should we receive $30,000 or more in funding, thereby meriting the expansion of the program to a size that needs dedicated staff, we will hire someone to fill that position and Colleen will act as supervisor.

The Georgia Center for Children provides a simple, straightforward staffing section.

Project Staff:

This project is directly administered by Center Psychotherapist, Pat Highsmith Lawyer. Pat has a M.S. in Counseling Psychology and previously worked in Child Protective Services for DeKalb County Department of Family and Children Services. She has received accolades from district attorneys, parents and children about the Court School program. In addition to conducting Court School, Pat also oversees all Center group therapy programs, conducts individual psychotherapy for sexually abused children, conducts the Center's Outreach Prevention Program, and coordinates the Center's Resource Referral Program.

Finally, the Center for Responsive Politics presents information about the board as well as key staff.

An active Board of Directors guides the Center's work. This board is led by two former members of Congress: Senator Dick Clark and Representative Orval Hansen. Until recently, Senator Hugh Scott, a founder of the Center, has also lent his considerable leadership and expertise to the Center. Other members of the Board include individuals with distinguished public service careers: Bethine Church, Peter Fenn, George Denison, Paul Hoff, Steven Hofman, Paul Thomas, Robert A. Weinberger and Executive Director Ellen Miller, as well as philanthropist Peter Kovler, and public relations executive Tim Brosnahan.

The Center's Executive Director—Ellen Miller—has extensive congressional experience, both as a senior staffer in both the House and Senate, and as a veteran of the public interest community in Washington. As Executive Director of the Center for Responsive Politics, she directs and manages all project areas: Money and Politics, Congressional Operations, Congress and the Media, Ethics in Government, and Foundations in Public Policy. In addition, as the Center's Executive Director for the past six years, she has been responsible for providing overall management, program planning, direction and fundraising and outreach for the organization. Ms. Miller is an expert on all aspects of the presidential and congressional campaign finance system, as well as on institutional issues concerning Congress. She has written and spoken extensively on money and politics issues, particularly on the rise of campaign spending over the past decade. She holds an advanced degree in urban and regional planning and has completed extensive studies in public policy research.

The Center's Senior Research Associate—Larry Makinson— will serve as Project Director for this project. One of the pioneers of computer research on campaign financing, he is the author of four books on the subject, including *Open Secrets: The Dollar Power of PACs in Congress* and *The Price of Admission: An Illustrated Atlas of Campaign Spending in the 1988 Congressional Elections.* As a longtime journalist in Alaska, Makinson won national awards for his reporting both in newspapers and public television. He holds a masters degree in public administration from the Kennedy School of Government at Harvard University.

Describe for the reader your plans for administering the project. This is especially important in a large operation, if more than one agency is collaborating on the project, or if you are using a fiscal agent. It needs to be crystal clear who is responsible for financial management, project outcomes, and reporting.

Evaluation

An evaluation plan should not be considered only after the project is over; it should be built into the project. Including an evaluation plan in your proposal indicates that you take your objectives seriously and want to know how well you have achieved them. Evaluation is also a sound management tool. Like strategic planning, it helps a non-profit refine and improve its program. An evaluation can often be the best means for others to learn from your experience in conducting the project.

Match the evaluation to the project. If you are asking for funds to buy an additional personal computer, it is not necessary to develop an elaborate plan to assess its impact on your operation. But if you have requested $100,000 to encourage people to have blood tests for Lyme disease, you should have a mechanism to determine whether the project's activities achieved your goals and objectives.

Many projects will have rather obvious evaluation procedures built into them. An art institution working on audience development, a settlement house providing an after-school program to disadvantaged children, or a health clinic offering preventive immunization will not spend a great deal of money and time evaluating their respective projects. The number of people served will be the major indicator of the success of these projects.

Not all funders require a formal evaluation; some want monitoring reports only. In this case, it is up to you to decide whether a formal evaluation is an essential component of the project.

The Contra Costa College excerpt cites specific outcomes and the related measurement for each.

Program Evaluation

The program will be evaluated by a team of three evaluators, at least one of which is on the staff of the Richmond Schools. Pre and post measures will be collected before and during their implementation of each component of the program. School records will also be used.

The following is a list of expected program outcomes, and measures to be used to assess them.

Outcome — Increased parent participation in the Metas program.
Measure — Did each parent bring a new family by the second year, thus doubling participation?

Outcome — Increased parent participation in school-generated activities.
Measure — Attendance at meetings, Back to School night, Open House, parent conferences, and participation on School Site Councils.

Outcome — Increased parent comfort with literacy (years 2 & 3).
Measure — Pre and post parent surveys and pre and post student surveys about parent literacy.

Outcome — Improved parent-teacher understanding.
Measure — Pre and post survey to teachers and parents.

Outcome — Improved student school performance.
Measure — Increased student attendance and improved grades.

End of Program Expected Outcome — Ensure that the project has provided a strong foundation such that the parents form and maintain an ongoing action coalition and remain involved in school site activities and strategic planning for educational improvement.

Note: Evaluation measuring each expected outcome will be collected each year, but significant gains are expected to accrue only over time. Therefore, the final program evaluation will be more reflective of the measurable success of the project than will the yearly evaluations.

Here is the evaluation section of a proposal by Recruiting New Teachers, Inc. submitted to the DeWitt Wallace–Reader's Digest Fund.

Evaluation

RNT will continue to use a combination of internal and external evaluation methods. The most important form of external evaluation has been the two national surveys of the RNT respondent pool, conducted by Louis Harris in 1990 and 1992. The objectives of both studies were to identify characteristics and attitudes of callers and to measure their progress into the profession. Both documents have been a critically important part of RNT's strategic planning, and have played crucial roles in suggesting, among other initiatives, the Urban Helpline and the *Careers in Teaching Handbook.* Another principal form of external evaluation, of course, has been the ongoing statistical tracking of response to the public service ad campaigns conducted by the Advertising Council and our telecommunications subcontractors.

Our ongoing evaluation efforts also include mail and telephone surveys to elicit feedback from RNT's institutional partner network; telephone surveys of selected groups of respondents; ongoing mail surveys of Urban Helpline callers to measure their reactions to the service and use of the resources offered them; ongoing tracking of Urban Helpline caller requests (number of calls daily, caller demographics, type of query, etc.) and resources provided; response (via business reply cards) to publications such as the Executive Summary of *Teaching's Next Generation,* RNT's report on its precollegiate teacher recruitment study; monitoring of response to education press accounts of RNT activities; occasional focus groups; reviews provided by such bodies as the Handbook's National Advisory Board; and post-conference evaluation forms.

To monitor both the usage rate and the effectiveness of each aspect of the RNT campaign, we will continue the various formative and summative, quantitative and qualitative, internal and external evaluation methods mentioned above. Whenever possible, new evaluation results will be compared to baseline data collected previously. For example, a third national study of the respondent pool in FY95–96* will allow results to be compared longitudinally with data from the 1990 and 1992 studies. This will help us to measure the effectiveness of the Outreach & Response campaign relative to our past experience, to pinpoint any changes in response from specific populations pursuing pathways into teaching, and to intervene accordingly. Campaign projects now in the final stages of the development process, such as the Spanish-language versions of RNT's print, radio, and TV ads, plus the *Careers in Teaching Handbook* (both forthcoming shortly) will be tested via focus groups and random user surveys, as well. This data is routinely analyzed and shared with our Board and funders in regularly prepared grant reports.

New activities to be undertaken as part of RNT's National Center on Precollegiate Teacher Recruitment will, of course, be evaluated in a similar manner. RNT will collect information on new and existing precollegiate programs and program models in order to update our print and computerized directories and facilitate the dissemination of that data in usable form to practitioners in the field. We will measure annually the numbers and types of requests for technical or other assistance and will solicit feedback on effectiveness from those who use our services. Most notably, by assisting program directors with development of their own assessment/evaluation tools (a near-universal program weakness identified during the 1992 RNT/DeWitt study of precollegiate teacher recruitment), the Center staff will enhance RNT's overall evaluation capabilities in the precollegiate programming area.

---

*In 1996–97 RNT is undertaking a pilot evaluation project geared to seek more accurate data on the progress of *specific* respondents on pathways into teaching through more detailed recruitment partner tracking and follow-up. Similarly, in response to frequent requests for program evaluation assistance from precollegiate programs, RNT is developing a common evaluation protocol and an introductory evaluation handbook for program directors (and others). The proposed handbook will also contain tools for assessing program components and monitoring outcomes.

The next excerpt from a proposal WomenVenture submitted to the General Mills Foundation combines self-evaluation and participation in outside evaluation.

Evaluation

WomenVenture has made a strong commitment to quality services. To ensure that its programs are of the highest quality and effectiveness, the agency follows a rigorous evaluation process. The organization collects data on clients and program outcomes, solicits client feedback and incorporates these findings into its program planning. Whenever possible, WomenVenture incorporates formal evaluation strategies into its special programs. For example, the SETO program has contracted with Wilder Research Center to evaluate the effectiveness of this program.

In addition, WomenVenture participates in the Self-Employment Learning Project (SELP), a longitudinal evaluation of microenterprise loan funds conducted by the Aspen Institute. Through this project, WomenVenture and six other agencies located across the country track the growth of microenterprises and evaluate the effectiveness of these programs as a poverty-alleviation strategy.

There are two types of formal evaluation. One measures the product; the other analyzes the process. Either or both might be appropriate to your project. The approach you choose will depend on the nature of the project and its objectives. For either type, you will need to describe the manner in which evaluation information will be collected and how the data will be analyzed. You should present your plan for how the evaluation and its results will be reported and the audiences to which it will be directed. For example, it might be used internally or be shared with the funder, or it might deserve a wider audience. A funder might have an opinion about the scope of this dissemination.

Should in-house staff or outside consultants conduct a formal evaluation? Staff may not have sufficient distance from the project to be objective. An outside person can bring objectivity to the project, but consultants may be costly and require time to learn about your agency and the project. Again, the nature of the project and of the evaluation may well determine the answer to this question. In any case, the evaluation needs to strike a balance between familiarity with the project and objectivity about the product or process.

6

Developing the Master Proposal: The Budget

The project description provides the picture of your proposal in words. The budget further refines that picture, but with numbers. A well-crafted budget adds greatly to the proposal reviewer's understanding of your project.

The budget for your proposal may be as simple as a one-page statement of projected expenses. Or your proposal may require a more complex presentation, perhaps including a page on projected support and revenue and notes explaining various items of expense or of revenue.

Expense Budget

As you prepare to assemble the budget, go back through the proposal narrative and make a list of all personnel and nonpersonnel items related to the operation of the project. Be sure that you list not only new costs that will be incurred if the project is funded but also any ongoing expenses for items that will be allocated to the project. Then get the relevant costs from the person in your agency who is responsible for keeping the books. You may need to estimate the proportions of your agency's ongoing expenses that should be charged to the project and any new costs, such as salaries for project personnel not yet hired. Put the costs you have identified next to each item on your list.

It is accepted practice to include as line items in your project budget any costs of the agency that will be specifically devoted to operating the project. Most commonly, these are the costs of supervision and of occupancy. If the project is large relative to the organization as a whole, these line items might also include telephone, utilities, office supplies, and similar expenses. For instance, if one of three office phone lines will be devoted to the project, one-third of the monthly cost of maintaining phone service could legitimately be listed as a project cost.

In addition, most expense budgets include a line called "overhead," which allows the project to bear a portion of the administrative costs, often called supporting services, of your operation. Such items as the bookkeeper's salary, board meeting expenses, the annual audit, and the cost of operating your personnel department might be included in the overhead figure. These costs are not directly attributable to the project but can be allocated to it based on the notion that the project should bear some of the costs of the host organization.

Most groups use a formula for allocating overhead costs to projects, usually based on the percentage of the total project budget to the total organizational budget or to its total salary line. For example, if the project budget is one-tenth the size of the total budget, it could be expected to bear one-tenth of the administrative overhead costs. Funders may have policies regarding the percentage of overhead that they will allow in a project budget. Some do not allow any overhead at all to be included. If possible, you should find out about the overhead policy before submitting your proposal to a particular foundation, because you may need to explain to that funder how you will cover overhead costs from other sources.

Your list of budget items and the calculations you have done to arrive at a dollar figure for each item should be summarized on worksheets. You should keep these to remind yourself how the numbers were developed. These worksheets can be useful as you continue to develop the proposal and discuss it with funders; they are also a valuable tool for monitoring the project once it is under way and for reporting after completion of the grant.

A portion of a worksheet for a year-long project might look like this:

Item	Description	Cost
Executive director	Supervision	10% of salary = $10,000 25% benefits = $2,500
Project director	Hired in month one	11 months full time at $35,000 = $32,083
Tutors	12 working 10 hours per week for 13 weeks	12 x 10 x 13 x $4.50 = $7,020
Office space	Requires 25% of current space	25% x $20,000 = $5,000
Overhead	20% of project cost	20% x $64,628 = $12,926

With your worksheets in hand, you are ready to prepare the expense budget. For most projects, costs should be grouped into subcategories, selected to reflect the critical areas of expense. All significant costs should be broken out within the subcategories, but small ones can be combined on one line. You might divide your expense budget into personnel and nonpersonnel costs. Personnel subcategories might include salaries, benefits, and consultants. Subcategories under nonpersonnel costs might include travel, equipment, and printing, for example, with a dollar figure attached to each line.

Two expense budgets follow. The first example, from Project Renewal, uses standard subcategories to group costs.

Project Renewal Inc.
Mobile Medical Outreach Clinic

EXPENSES

Personnel

Physician (part-time)	$ 31,286
Mid-Level Nurse Practitioner	55,000
Social Worker	40,000
Aide/Driver	32,503
Medical Director (10%)	11,268
Secretary	26,751
Total Personnel	$196,808
Fringe Benefits	$ 63,055

Other than Personnel Services

Lab Fees	$3,426
Medical Supplies	24,667
Patient Supplies	1,370
Fuel	8,469
Garage Rental	7,948
Van Rental	4,111
Vehicle Maintenance	13,389
Equipment Rental	2,056
Insurance	19,761
Office Supplies	582
Membership Dues	2,056
Recruiting	8,469
Telephone	6,167
Travel	1,370
Total Other than Personnel Services	$103,841
Total Expense	**$363,704**

The next budget, from the Cleveland Institute of Art, uses non-standard subcategories that are consistent with the project.

Cleveland Institute of Art
Proposal to The Cleveland Foundation

Budget

I. Consultant

Honorarium (6 visits x $2,000)	$12,000
Airfare (6 trips x $300)	1,800
Lodging (6 visits x 4 nights x $100)	2,400
Per Diem (6 visits x 4 days x $40)	960
Subtotal	$17,160

II. Faculty Honoraria

New Participants (8 x 12 sessions x $100)	$9,600
Past Participants (5 x 6 sessions x $100)	3,000
Administrative Coordinator	3,000
Subtotal	$15,600

III. Curriculum Redesign

Faculty Stipends (3 x $1,500)	$4,500
Release Time (3 visiting faculty x $5,000 for one course)	15,000
Subtotal	$19,500

IV. Workshops Meals

Lunches (17 members x 6 sessions x $10)	$1,020
Lunches (12 members x 6 sessions x $10)	720
Subtotal	$1,740

Total	**$54,000**

Support and Revenue Statement

For the typical project, no support and revenue statement is necessary. The expense budget represents the amount of grant support required. But if grant support has already been awarded to the project, or if you expect project activities to generate income, a support and revenue statement is the place to provide this information.

In itemizing grant support, make note of any earmarked grants; this will suggest how new grants may be allocated. The total grant support already committed should then be deducted from the "Total Expenses" line on the expense budget to give you the "Amount to Be Raised" or the "Balance Requested."

Any earned income anticipated should be estimated on the support and revenue statement. For instance, if you expect 50 people to attend your performance on each of the four nights it is given at $10 a ticket, and if you hope that 20 of them will buy the $5 souvenir book each night, you would show two lines of income, "Ticket Sales" at $2,000 and "Souvenir Book Sales" at $400. As with the expense budget, you should keep backup worksheets for the support and revenue statement to remind yourself of the assumptions you have made.

Because an earned income statement deals with anticipated revenues, rather than grant commitments in hand, the difference between expenses and revenues is usually labeled "Balance Requested," rather than "Amount to Be Raised." The funder will appreciate your recognition that the project will earn even a small amount of money—and might well raise questions about this if you do not include it in your budget.

Now that your budget is complete, take the time to analyze it objectively. Be certain that it is neither too lean nor on the high side in the expense estimates. If you estimate too closely, you may not be able to operate within the budget. You will have to go back to funders already supporting the project for additional assistance, seek new donors, or underwrite part of the cost out of general operating funds. None of these alternatives is attractive.

Consistently overestimating costs can lead to other problems. The donor awards a grant expecting that all of the funds will support the project, and most will instruct you to return any funds remaining at the end. If you have a lot of money left over, it will reflect badly on your budgeting ability. This will affect the funder's attitude toward any future budgets you might present.

Finally, be realistic about the size of your project and its budget. You will probably be including a copy of the organization's financial statements in the appendix for your proposal. A red flag will be raised with the proposal reviewer if the budget for a new project rivals the size of the rest of your operation.

If you are inexperienced in developing proposal budgets, you should ask your treasurer or someone who has successfully managed grant funds to review it for you. This can help you spot obvious problems that need to be fixed, and it can prepare you to answer questions that proposal reviewers might raise, even if you decide not to change the budget.

Budget Narrative

A budget narrative portion is used to explain any unusual line items in the budget and is not always needed. If costs are straightforward and the numbers tell the story clearly, explanations are redundant.

If you decide a budget narrative is needed, you can structure it in one of two ways. You can create "Notes to the Budget," with footnote-style numbers on the line items in the budget keyed to numbered explanations. Or, if an extensive or more general explanation is required, you can structure the budget narrative as straight text. Remember, though, that the basic narrative about the project and your organization belong elsewhere in the proposal, not in the budget narrative.

The following is an example of a budget with a narrative from the Phillis Wheatley Association. It is structured to indicate that the nonprofit is assuming part of the cost of the project.

Phillis Wheatley Association

1996 Budget

	Support Requested	PWA Contribution
Community Organizer/Administrative Assistant	$22,000	$ 5,000
Fringe Benefits @ 15%	4,500	—
2 Computers and 1 Printer	—	6,500
Professional Development/Training	2,500	3,500
Total	$29,000	$15,000
Grand Total		**$44,500**

Budget Narrative

1. Community Organizer/Administrative Assistant: support for salary over one year at $27,000.

2. Fringe Benefits: FICA, workers' compensation, health benefits and life insurance at $4,500.

3. Two Computers and one printer for use by the Executive Director and Community Organizer/Administrative Assistant. Computers at $2,500 apiece ($5,000) and a HP Laser jet printer at $1,500.

4. Professional Development and Inservice Training: primarily for current administrative staff; continued support for Neighborhood Leadership Cleveland graduates; support for computer training.

The finalized budget, whether one page or several, is now ready to include in the proposal document. Keep a copy of it with your backup worksheets in a special folder. The materials in this folder will assist you in tracking actual expenses as the project unfolds. They will enable you to anticipate lines that will go over budget or areas where you might have extra funds to spend, so that you can manage effectively the grant funds that you receive. These materials will also be extremely helpful when it comes time to write the grant report.

7

Developing the Master Proposal: Organization Information and Conclusion

Organization Information

Normally the resume of your nonprofit organization should come at the end of your proposal. Your natural inclination may be to put this information up front in the document, but it is usually better first to sell the need for your project and *then* your agency's ability to carry it out.

It is not necessary to overwhelm the reader with facts about your organization. This information can be conveyed easily by attaching a brochure or other prepared statement. In two pages or less, tell the reader when your nonprofit came into existence; state its mission, being certain to demonstrate how the subject of the proposal fits within or extends that mission; and describe the organization's structure, programs, and special expertise. The following example is taken from the proposal of the Phillis Wheatley Association. It is a summary of the history and responsiveness of this organization.

The Phillis Wheatley Association

Upon arriving in Cleveland from the South in 1905, Jane Edna Hunter experienced great difficulty finding adequate, inexpensive housing. Her personal experience motivated her to start the Working Girls Home Association to provide housing to young African American women new to Cleveland. In 1911, the Working Girls Home Association name was changed to the Phillis Wheatley Association (PWA) in honor of the first African American woman poet. The present [building housing] the Phillis Wheatley Association, located at East 46th Street and Cedar Avenue, was constructed in 1907.

The Phillis Wheatley Association has a history of adapting to the changing needs of the community. During the 1930s and 1940s, the PWA was a prominent meeting place for leaders in the African American community. The Phillis Wheatley Association not only offered a gathering place for social events, but provided music and dance lessons through its Stupen Music School. The PWA also assisted working families when its Josephine Kohler Day Care Center opened in 1937, and provided recreational alternatives to African American youngsters outside the urban area when Camp Mueller, a residential camp, was founded in 1938. From its change of residents from young women to the elderly, to its profound change in 1967 from what many referred to as the "black YWCA" to a neighborhood center, the Phillis Wheatley Association remains an important community resource.

Today, Camp Mueller remains the only African American owned camp in Ohio. The Camp continues to operate a summer day camp and serves as the primary training facility for the Rites of Passage movement underway in the Cleveland community and schools. The Rites of Passage effort spearheaded by Paul Hill, Executive Director of the East End Neighborhood House, represents a major move on the part of the PWA and other Neighborhood Center Association (NCA) centers to pool resources in support of the community and particularly its youth. Efforts to expand the use of the camp to the broader community will be a major focus of the PWA renaissance in 1996.

Discuss the size of the board, how board members are recruited, and their level of participation. Give the reader a feel for the makeup of the board. (You should include the full board list in the appendix.) If your agency is composed of volunteers or has an active volunteer group, describe the functions that the volunteers fill. Provide details on the staff, including numbers of full- and part-time staff and their levels of expertise.

Describe the kinds of activities in which your staff engage. Explain briefly the assistance you provide. Describe the audiences you serve, any special or unusual needs they face, and why they rely on your agency. Cite the number of people who are reached through your programs.

Tying all of the information about your nonprofit together, cite your agency's expertise, especially as it relates to the subject of your proposal.

This information, coupled with the attachments you will supply in the appendix, is all the funder will require at this stage. Keep in mind that funders may wish to check with other sources to help evaluate your organization and its expertise.

These sources might include experts in the field, contacts established at organizations similar to your own, other funders, or even agencies such as the Council of Better Business Bureaus' Philanthropic Advisory Service or the National Charities Information Bureau, which issue reports on some of the larger, national groups.

In the next sample, the Center for Families and Children describes itself and a merger partner, Reach Out.

Center for Families and Children

The Center for Families and Children (CFC) was created in 1970 as the Center for Human Services when five separate social service agencies—The Family Service Association, the Day Nursery Association, Homemaker Services, Youth Services and Traveler's Aid—were joined into one to provide a broader range of services under a centralized and more cost efficient administration. Dedicated to excellence in services to Youth, Child Day Care, HomeCare, Mental Health and Counseling, the Center operates 19 sites throughout the Greater Cleveland area, as well as in-home services to persons requiring such services. The Center changed its name in 1993 to the Center for Families and Children.

The Center's mission, as adopted by its board of trustees, states that the agency is "committed to excellence in sustaining and enhancing human potential and emotional well-being through programs designed to maintain families and individuals." The agency continues its ongoing commitment to the needs of low-income and minority groups. In short, the Center's primary objective is to help families, children, youth, and adults to remain or become self-sufficient, productive, and contributing members of the Greater Cleveland community. The Center is governed by a 42 member board of trustees which is reflective of the Greater Cleveland community. In 1994, the Center served over 11,000 clients with a staff of 280 and an annual budget of approximately $12 million dollars. As a private non-profit agency, CFC is funded by a variety of sources including the State of Ohio, United Way Services, Cuyahoga County, individuals, foundations, corporations, and by fees for services from corporate and individual clients. Charges for services to individuals are calculated on a sliding scale based on the client's income or ability to pay. Over the years, the Center has added a number of important community services such as the AIDS Initiative and the Grand Parent Support program, in response to charging community needs.

Reach Out

Reach Out is a social service agency based in Solon, Ohio. Organized in 1970 and supported through the United Way Services, Reach Out's primary mission is to provide individual and family counseling and education services to prevent substance abuse and to promote mental health. A special emphasis of Reach Out is to serve adolescents, adults, and families within the Greater Solon area, who, for financial reasons, find it difficult to obtain counseling services. Reach Out's mission also focuses on promoting a psychologically safe and growth-producing environment in the community it serves. Efforts are made to further this goal through consultation with community groups and individuals, and advocacy to public decision-makers for services to meet client needs.

Reach Out has an annual budget of $400,000. Financial support is derived from the following sources: Alcohol and Drug Board; United Way Services; the City of Solon; program service fees; and finally contributions and donations.

Prior to the merger, Reach Out was governed by a 10 member board of trustees which had representation from a variety of sectors in the Greater Solon community. The program has traditionally employed a staff of six full-time and part-time employees who were not organized in a bargaining unit in contrast to the Center for Families and Children. Reach Out serves approximately 600 clients per year.

Conclusion

Every proposal should have a concluding paragraph or two. This is a good place to call attention to the future, after the grant is completed. If appropriate, you should outline some of the follow-up activities that might be undertaken, to begin to prepare your funders for your next request. Alternatively, you should state how the project might carry on without further grant support.

This section is also the place to make a final appeal for your project. Briefly reiterate what your nonprofit wants to do and why it is important. Underscore why your agency needs funding to accomplish it. Don't be afraid at this stage to use a bit of emotion to solidify your case.

Three examples follow. The first is the conclusion to a proposal from the East Side House Settlement. It is a strong restatement of the facts that appeared in the body of the proposal.

Conclusion

East Side House requests $90,000 over three years from the Henry Luce Foundation to provide 50 young adults annually with literacy, math and parenting skills adequate to break the cycle of dependence. These young parents are working to prepare themselves for employment. They are also articulate about wanting a better life for their children. The Family Literacy Program helps them build basic skills in math, writing and reading while also building parenting skills. It addresses their need to balance their efforts to launch their own lives as employed adults with their efforts to become pro-active, able parents.

Now entering its third year, the Family Literacy Program has become known to other parents enrolled in the Educational Services Program. They see its value and want to join. Because the Program collaborates with other community agencies, as well as drawing on the larger resources of East Side House core staff and services, its costs are very modest.

We are ready to expand this program from 30 to 50 young adults. We need to continue evaluation and program revision for at least two more annual cycles, and then institutionalize the project in the third year as part of the core offerings of East Side House. Henry Luce Foundation support will assure that these goals are met.

The second is the conclusion to a proposal developed by Mind-Builders Family Services Center. It is simple and straightforward.

Conclusion

Mind-Builders Family Services Center is an essential addition to Mind-Builders' services to residents of the northeast Bronx. Since 1978, our community has against many odds pulled together to establish Mind-Builders as a source of creativity and community. The Family Services Center is Mind-Builders response to social conditions that threaten the stability of our families and children. By empowering young women to build positive lives free from alcohol and drug abuse, Mind-Builders is helping to ensure healthy environments for children and a future for the community.

The final example is from a proposal of the Brooklyn Children's Museum. It is quite inspirational.

The Brooklyn Children's Museum continues to balance its unique national leadership roll in the field of children's museums with a commitment to its community of Crown Heights, to its home borough of Brooklyn and to the city of New York. An institution can only achieve such a unique balance when there is a common goal and interest. Here, at BCM, the common goal and interest is children and our mission to help them ". . . understand and respect themselves, each other and the natural world."

The Museum Team program represents—in many ways—the creative partnership BCM strives to build with children and its community. By involving children in creating the program instead of merely offering a menu of staff-created services, we are laying the valuable cornerstones of leadership, responsibility to self and others, and community pride so important to youngsters and teens.

Museum Team would not be possible without the support and partnership with our many generous donors. We hope you will be able to join us this year to reach hundreds of youngsters in Crown Heights and Bedford-Stuyvesant through this unique and innovative program.

8

Variations on the Master Proposal Format

In the preceding chapters we presented the recommended format for components of the standard proposal. In reality, however, not every proposal will slavishly adhere to these guidelines. This should not be surprising. Sometimes the scale of the project might suggest a small-scale proposal to match, or the type of request might not require all of the proposal components or the components in the sequence recommended here. The guidelines and policies of individual funders will be your ultimate guide. Some funders state that they prefer a brief letter proposal; others require that you complete an application form. In any case, you will want to refer to the basic proposal components (see Chapter 2) to be sure that you have not omitted an element that will support your case.

What follows is a description of a letter proposal and of other format variations.

A Letter Proposal

The scale of the project will often determine whether it requires a letter or the longer proposal format. For example, a request to purchase a $1,000 fax machine for your agency simply does not lend itself to a lengthy narrative. A small contribution to your agency's annual operating budget, particularly if it is a renewal of past support, might also warrant a letter rather than a full-scale proposal.

What are the elements of a letter request? For the most part, they should follow the format of a full proposal, except with regard to length. The letter should be no more than three pages. You will need to call upon your writing skills because it can be very hard to get all of the necessary details into a concise, well-articulated letter.

As to the flow of information, follow these steps while keeping in mind that you are writing a letter to someone. It should not be as formal in style as a longer proposal would be. It may be necessary to change the sequence of the text to achieve the correct tone and the right flow of information.

Here are the components of a good letter proposal, with excerpts of relevant sections of a letter proposal from the Edenwald-Gun Hill Neighborhood Center.

Ask for the gift: The letter should begin with a reference to your prior contact with the funder, if any. State why you are writing and how much funding is required from the particular foundation.

Dear Dr. _____ :

I am writing to the Foundation regarding a much needed pilot project for the parents and children of the Edenwald Housing Projects and surrounding area. Edenwald's new Parenting Program will address the special needs of low-income young mothers ages 14–28 and their families. The Parenting Program will help young women to build strong and healthy families.

XXX has provided a generous grant of $25,000 to enable Edenwald to hire a social worker who will begin the Parenting Program early this fall. It is my hope that the Foundation will also support Edenwald's efforts to implement the Parenting Program by providing a grant of $10,000 to help underwrite the costs of the salaries of the Outreach and Child Care Workers.

Describe the need: In a very abbreviated manner, tell the funder why there is a need for this project, piece of equipment, etc.

Almost half the families that reside in the Edenwald Public Housing Complex are headed by single parents, and over one third live on public assistance. There is a pressing need in the community served by Edenwald for programs and activities that help our children to achieve in school and reach their full potential. Each year hundreds of youth drop out of area high schools. A vast majority of children served by Edenwald test below grade level in reading and math. Unfortunately, Edenwald staff have also witnessed an alarming increase in the number of young girls from our service area giving birth to children.

Most of these young women are unprepared to cope with the financial or the emotional demands of raising a family. While we recognize teen pregnancy prevention education is greatly needed in our community, a pressing and immediate demand exists for a program that will help these young parents raise healthy children. As government cutbacks, crime and unemployment continue to increase in urban areas, so do the odds against our children growing-up to be healthy and successful. To many parents from our service area, Edenwald has become a source of hope for the future of their children by giving them the educational support and services that they alone cannot provide. The Parenting Program will be an important addition to Edenwald's efforts to strengthen our families and community.

Edenwald-Gun Hill Neighborhood Center serves children that reside in the Edenwald Housing Project, as well as other community youngsters. The population served is 60% African-American and 40% Latino. Edenwald is located in a rough drug infested area. Because of the deteriorating conditions of the northeast Bronx an increasing number of children and youth are at-risk. Approximately 79% of the arrests made in the local precinct are for crimes committed by youth ages 10–25 years old. Edenwald Houses has a population of 9,000 residents. More than 5,000 of the residents are young people between the ages of one month and 21 years.

Explain what you will do: Just as you would in a fuller proposal, provide enough detail to pique the funder's interest. Describe precisely what will take place as a result of the grant.

The Parenting Program will serve approximately 25 young mothers between the ages 14–28. Some of these women will be teens who have recently given birth and need basic information about child rearing. Other women who will enroll in the program already participate in Edenwald activities and have children as old as three, but have never received instruction in parenting and want to increase their knowledge and sophistication about child care issues.

Parenting Program Goals

Edenwald-Gun Hill Neighborhood Center recognizes the importance of bringing together youngsters, parents and community members whose involvement is essential to the healthy development of our children. By building a network of encouragement and support, the Parenting Program will help ensure that children receive the care they need to grow into healthy adults. The goals of the Parenting Program are to:

- provide parents with the knowledge they need in order to deal with the demands of parenthood
- increase the self-esteem of parents
- help build strong, positive relationships between parents and children
- teach parents the importance of becoming active participants in their child's growth and education
- encourage parents to take charge of their lives and plan for the future of themselves and their families

Methodology

By utilizing a combination of group discussions, individual meetings and case management the Parenting Program seeks to address the developmental needs of mothers and children of different ages. Individual meetings with parents will enable staff to address the specific developmental needs of parents and children. Parents will be encouraged to focus on their own dreams, obstacles and the need to take responsibility for themselves and their children.

The Parenting Program will operate throughout the year. An Outreach Worker will be responsible for coordinating and overseeing the administration of the program. A Social Worker will design, plan and lead the Parenting Program sessions. The Social Worker will hold weekly support groups and individual sessions for parents and oversee case management. The Outreach Worker will conduct outreach and recruitment for the program, work with the Social Worker and help perform case management and follow-up on behalf of program participants. The Outreach worker will be responsible for arranging linkages with other local social services agencies and will also provide referrals. The Child Care Worker will be on hand to work with and supervise the children while their parents receive program services. In addition, the Child Care Worker will assist the Social Worker in helping to teach parents how to best care for their children.

The Social Worker will lead discussions that will help program participants to understand important child development issues such as: understanding and coping with a child's sleep habits; how to handle a crying infant; setting limits; dealing with fears; social development; and toilet readiness. Discussion topics will also help to ease a parent's transition to parenthood by addressing topics including: a parent's feelings of isolation; understanding changes in wife/husband relationship; coping with fatigue; and dealing with anger, frustration and anxiety as a parent.

Provide agency data: Help the funder know a bit more about your organization by including your mission statement, brief description of programs offered, number of people served, and staff, volunteer, and board data, if appropriate

History and Mission

Edenwald's mission is to strengthen the families in our community by providing an array of activities. Our goals are to ensure that young people develop the skills and self esteem needed to succeed and to ensure that parents receive the services they need to keep their families healthy and productive.

During the mid 1970's, it became clear that children and adolescents at the Edenwald Housing Project needed a neighborhood center to provide an alternative to the gangs that began to emerge in the project. In 1974, the Tenants Association succeeded in persuading the Housing Authority to provide space for a private group to set up a community center, and United Neighborhood Houses established the Edenwald-Gun Hill Neighborhood Center.

Include appropriate budget data: Even a letter request may have a budget that is half a page long. Decide if this information should be incorporated into the letter or in a separate attachment. Whichever course you choose, be sure to indicate the total cost of the project. Discuss future funding only if the absence of this information will raise questions.

Close: As with the longer proposal, a letter proposal needs a strong concluding statement.

Conclusion

The support of the Foundation will help ensure that Edenwald is able to provide vital assistance that promotes the healthy development of our children and hope for the future of our community. It is our hope that the Foundation will provide a grant of $10,000 to help initiate a Parenting Program for young mothers. The grant will be used to underwrite the salaries of the Outreach and Child Care Workers for one year.

Enclosed please find documents supporting this request. Please call me if you have any questions, or if you would like to arrange to visit Edenwald.

Thank you for your interest in our work.

Attach any additional information required: The funder may need much of the same information to back up a small request as a large one: a board list, a copy of your IRS determination letter, financial documentation, and brief résumés of key staff. Rather than preparing a separate appendix, you should list the attachments at the end of a letter proposal, following the signature.

It may take as much thinking and data gathering to write a good letter request as it does to write a full proposal (and sometimes even more). Don't assume that because it is only a letter, it isn't a time-consuming and challenging task. Every document you put in front of a funder says something about your agency. Each step you take with a funder should build a relationship for the future.

Other Variations in Format

Just as the scale of the project will dictate whether a letter or a full proposal is used, so the type of request will be the determining factor as to whether all of the components of a full proposal are required.

The following section will explore the information that should appear in the proposal application for five different types of requests: special project, general purpose, capital, endowment, and purchase of equipment.

Special Project

The basic proposal format presented in earlier chapters uses the special project proposal as the prototype because this is the type of proposal that you will most often be required to design. As stated previously, funders tend to prefer to make grants for specific projects because such projects are finite and tangible, and their results are measurable. Most special project proposals will follow this format, or these basic components will be developed in a letter.

General Purpose

A general purpose proposal requests operating support for your agency. Therefore, it focuses more broadly on your organization, rather than on a specific project. All of the information in the standard proposal should be present, but there will not be a separate component describing your organization. That information will be the main thrust of the entire proposal. Also, your proposal budget will be the budget for the entire organization, so it need not be duplicated in the appendix.

Two components of the general purpose proposal deserve special attention. They are the need statement and program information, which replaces the "project description" component. The need section is especially important. You must make the case for your nonprofit organization itself, and you must do it succinctly. What are the circumstances that led to the creation of your agency? Are those circumstances still urgent today? Use language that involves the reader, but be logical in the presentation of supporting data. For example, a local organization should cite local statistics, not national ones.

The following is an example of a need statement from a general purpose proposal for the Kenmare High School in Jersey City, New Jersey.

Kenmare High School is an alternative learning experience for young women who are not able to continue in a traditional school setting. In Gaelic, Kenmare means "nest." The school was established to reflect that definition, to be a nurturing place where students receive skills instruction in a supportive and communal environment. Founded by the Sisters of Saint Joseph of Peace in 1982, Kenmare serves the young women of Hudson County, and especially those in the downtown area of Jersey City. Any woman, regardless of race or creed, aged 16 to 25, who has dropped out of a traditional school setting is eligible for enrollment.

The Women We Serve

The 80 students who currently attend Kenmare mirror the ever increasing female population whose life situations reflect the harsh reality of the feminization of poverty. Sixty-five percent of the student body at Kenmare are mothers with an average of two children per family. Of these families, 53% are female-headed, single parent households. Sixty-three percent of the women receive some form of public assistance, while the remainder are considered working poor. The current student body at Kenmare is 60% Black and 40% Hispanic. The sum total of their experiences reveal stories of deep personal losses, racism, sexism and constant emotional strains. The women that enroll in Kenmare are seeking an alternative to their current lifestyles.

Why Kenmare is Unique

Through a unique and holistic approach to education, Kenmare offers a program that addresses the academic, career and personal needs of these young women. Because Kenmare students usually have responsibilities in addition to school—parenting or support of families—the program is designed to be as flexible as possible while maintaining high instructional standards. For example, students will be excused to take their children to doctors, to attend parent–teacher conferences for their pre-schoolers, or to go to court for child support. The school provides a nurturing environment with individualized programs and small group classes, which never exceed ten students. All staff efforts are designed to meet the needs of students whose success requires intensive staff time and attention.

Consider including details on recent accomplishments and future directions as seen in this excerpt from a request to the J. P. Morgan Charitable Trust by Project Reach Youth. The original proposal contained 13 points of which five are presented here.

Recent Accomplishments and Future Directions Include:

A) Second annual Project Reach Youth **Teen Conference,** "Breaking Down the Walls, Conflict in the 90's", in April, 1994, led by teens for teens focusing on the issue of violence in our communities. Over 200 young people attended the conference, as well as elected officials, to discuss various topics related to violence. Our plan is to continue this important leadership development activity, with an additional focus on community service.

B) Implementation of several elements of our **community school partnership** with Public School 124, located next door. Last spring, PRY teachers and tutors started providing in-school tutoring to small groups of 28 academically at-risk first graders. Last summer, PRY opened a licensed pre-school for 15 four year olds who will begin kindergarten at PS 124 in the fall of 1994 which will be expanded to include a second session, 3 afternoons in the fall of 1994. The program offers an enriched early childhood curriculum for the children with simultaneous parenting workshops and adult education for their parents. We will be expanding this pre-school program to two sessions (morning and afternoon) per day. Beginning this fall, PRY is offering after-school enrichment activities in math and science for 30 PS 124 students who are on grade level but could benefit from additional academic stimulation. This fall will also see the beginning of our 1st grade reading program and English as a Second Language instruction for students who need these services.

C) The expansion of our **AIDS peer education program** to include a support group for teens dealing with AIDS in their families. We have continued to expand our Immigrant Youth SAFE program for 20 immigrant youth teens to educate their Spanish speaking peers about HIV and AIDS prevention. In addition, we have just received funding to work with extremely hard to reach populations including out-of-school youth and teen parents. With the help of additional funding, we have translated our extremely popular and informative "Teens' Guide to AIDS" into Spanish. The new guide will be going to press shortly.

D) This past year has seen the launching of our efforts at one of New York City's **Beacon Schools,** designed to utilize public schools as community centers, open all day, during the evenings and on weekends, offering comprehensive academic and social services for children and families. Project Reach Youth has been selected to provide academic remediation, English as a Second Language classes, Spanish literacy and acculturation programs for recent immigrants and other children and their families.

E) The development and implementation of a **conflict mediation and violence prevention program** for teens which began this winter using a peer education model.

Capital

A capital proposal requests funds for facility purchase, construction, or renovation, or possibly land purchase or long-term physical plant improvements. Today many institutions include other items in a capital campaign, such as endowment funds, program expansion, and salaries for professors. But, for our purposes, we will discuss the more traditional definition of capital, that is, "bricks and mortar."

All of the components of a proposal will be included in a capital request. Differences in content will mainly be in the need statement, the project description, the budget, and the appendix.

The need section in the capital proposal should focus on why the construction or renovation is required. The challenge is to make the programs that will use the facility come alive to the reader. For example, your agency may need to expand its day care program because of the tremendous need in your community among working parents for such support, the long waiting list you have, and the potential educational value to the child. Your proposal will be less compelling if the focus of the need statement is purely related to space considerations or to meeting code requirements.

Following is an excerpt from a capital proposal for the Summit Area (NJ) YMCA.

The Need

A policy to respond proactively to the region's demographics drives this expansion. At first glance, Summit appears the stable, comfortable community it was laid out to be in the last century. It has diminished slightly in size between 1980 and 1990 as the trend toward later marriages and smaller families continues. Its population is dominated by families, young adults, active older adults whose families have grown, and senior citizens. But Summit's internal demographic shifts over the last decade are significant. Each one represents changing regional needs to which the Y is uniquely positioned to respond.

1) Census data reveals a 28.7% jump in pre-schoolers for 1980 to 1990. This trend continues in the first half of the 1990's, putting increasing pressure on child care and enrichment resources for young children and their families. The number of students in the Summit School

---

system is projected to increase by over 700 by the year 2000.

2) A 33.5% drop in school age youth lead to reduced public school and recreation programming. The sudden rise in service demand as pre-schoolers reach school age has stressed schools and community organizations alike.

3) At the same time, the number of adults aged 45 to 64 dropped 11.6% as downsizing corporations transferred or eliminated management-level employees, and others moved out of town to smaller living quarters. Within this age group still living in town, more two-earner couples can be found than ever before. The net result is a significant loss in time available for community volunteer effort and care of elderly parents and grandchildren.

4) Reflecting advances in geriatric care, those 85 and older rose 13.6%.

5) Summit's income diversity is increasing. Young couples and families moving into Summit's most expensive homes have higher median incomes than the older couples they replace. Meanwhile, modestly-priced rental property continues to draw singles and families with lower incomes.

During this period, the region mirrored the larger New Jersey trends of increased ethnic and cultural diversity.

1) Traditional white and black population segments dropped as those who moved away were replaced by other ethnic groups. (Non-Hispanic white dropped 9.9% and black dropped 7.8%) Even within these traditional populations, households identifying themselves as Jewish and Islamic increased, so that diversity increased. There are currently over 35 languages spoken in the homes of Summit students.

2) The Asian population grew 135%. Ranging from young highly educated professionals to immigrant households of limited means, this group challenges the Summit region with its desires for amenities and needs for specialized services.

3) The Hispanic population grew 57.7%, again presenting great diversity in household resources and resulting service needs.

4) The total minority population in Summit grew from 10.8% in 1980 to 15.1% in 1990. The Summit Housing Authority reports that this trend continues.

5) In five years, the Y has gone from awarding $60,000 to over $135,000 in annual financial assistance to individuals and families who wish to join and participate in Y membership and activities but can not afford them.

While Summit continues to be dominated by family households, fully half of them are married without children. Because of the presence of high quality housing stock for singles, 80% of Summit's non-family households are single, mostly young adults.

This data tells an explicit story of the need for high volume, highly specialized services for pre-schoolers and young families, young adults, minorities and aged seniors. Summit leadership is aware of this data. Area residents interviewed for the Y's 1994 Feasibility Study recognized that Summit's public and community service institutions must respond to this changing community profile. The Y was cited repeatedly as "one of the few community organizations well positioned to respond to the demographic changes taking place in Summit." The diversity of age, economics, and ethnicity which come together was also noted in comments like, "It's the only place I can think of where all ages, all groups, come together around common interests."

The project description component of a capital proposal includes two elements. The first is the description of how your programs will be enhanced or altered as a result of the physical work. Then should come a description of the physical work itself. The funder is being asked to pay for the latter and should have a complete narrative on the work to be undertaken. You might supplement that description with drawings, if available. These could be external views of the facility, as well as interior sketches showing people using the facility. Floor plans might help as well. These need not be formal renderings by an artist or an architect; a well-drawn diagram will often make the case. Photos showing "before" and drawings indicating what the "after" will be like are also dramatic adjuncts to the capital proposal.

The budget for a capital proposal will be a very detailed delineation of all costs related to the construction, renovation, etc. It should include the following:

- actual brick and mortar expenses. These should be presented in some logical sequence related to the work being undertaken. For example, a renovation project might follow an area-by-area description, or a construction project might be presented chronologically. Don't forget to include expenses for such items as construction permits in this section.

- other costs: salaries, fees, and related expenses required to undertake the capital improvements. Be certain to include in your budget the projected costs of architects, lawyers, and public relations and fundraising professionals. Many capital proposal writers fail to adequately anticipate such "soft" costs.

- contingency: Estimates for actual construction costs often change during the fundraising and preconstruction periods. It is therefore a good idea to build a contingency into the budget in case costs exceed the budgeted amounts. A contingency of 10 to 20 percent is the norm; more than that tends to raise a proposal reviewer's eyebrows.

Here is an excerpt from a capital campaign budget for Planned Parenthood of Westchester & Rockland, Inc., New York:

Planned Parenthood of Westchester & Rockland, Inc.

<u>PROJECT BUDGET</u>

The Yonkers Center

Purchase/lease and renovate 12,000 sq. ft.	$1,000,000
Equip offices, medical and education space	205,000
Professional fees for design and licensing	71,000
Net increase in operating costs ($167,000/year for 3 years)	500,000
Recruit and train additional health care providers, including on-site Medical Director	165,000
Subtotal	$1,941,000

Increased Services in Central Westchester

Refit existing Tarrytown Road facility to increase medical capacity	$ 225,000
Purchase/lease and renovate 5,000 sq. ft. administrative office	270,000
Equip offices and medical area	20,000
Professional design & licensing	25,000
Net increase in operating costs ($82,000/year for 3 years)	246,000
Subtotal	$ 786,000

Security Refinements in all Nine Centers

Facility renovations	$60,000
Guard services ($55,000/year for 3 years)	165,000
Staff training	7,500
Subtotal	$ 232,500

Outreach

Double current endowment to $1,200,000 to subsidize fees for poor women	$600,000
Increase community education, outreach and training activities ($45,000/year for 3 years)	135,000
Subtotal	$ 735,000
Campaign Costs	$ 100,000
Grand Total	**$3,794,500**

The appendix to a capital proposal may be expanded to include floor plans and renderings if they do not appear within the proposal text. If a brochure has been developed in conjunction with the capital campaign, this could be sent along as part of the appendix package.

Endowment

An endowment is used by nonprofits to provide financial stability and to supplement grant and earned income. Often campaigns, designed like capital drives, are mounted to attract endowment dollars. A proposal specifically requesting funding for endowment may resemble either a special project or a general operating application, depending on whether the endowment is for a special purpose, such as scholarships or faculty salaries, or for the organization's general operations. Your focus will be on the following components: the need statement, the program description, and the budget.

The need statement for an endowment proposal will highlight why the organization must establish or add to its endowment. Points to raise might include:

- the importance of having available the interest from the endowment's corpus as an adjunct to the operating budget;
- the desire to stabilize annual income, which is currently subject to the vagaries of government grants;
- the value of endowing a particular activity of your organization that lacks the capacity to earn income or attract gift support.

The program description will cover the impact of endowment dollars on the programs of your nonprofit. Provide as many details as possible in explaining the direct consequences of these dollars. Indicate if there are naming or memorial opportunities as part of the endowment fund.

The budget will round out all of this data by indicating how much you are trying to raise and in what categories. For example, there might be a need to endow 75 scholarships at $10,000 each for a total of $750,000.

Equipment

Frequently, organizations have a need to develop a free-standing proposal for purchase of a piece of equipment, be it MRI equipment for a hospital or a personal computer for an ongoing program. These would require only a letter proposal, but the scale or significance of the purchase may dictate a full proposal. Again, the need statement, the project description, and the budget will be primary.

In the need statement, explain why the organization must have this equipment. For example, this hospital has no MRI equipment, and people in the community have to travel great distances when an MRI test is required.

Then in the project description, explain how the equipment will alter the way services are delivered. For example: "The new MRI equipment will serve some 500 people annually. It will assist in diagnoses ranging from structural problems in the foot to tracking the development of a lung tumor. The cost per procedure will be $1,000, but it will save millions in unnecessary surgical procedures."

This budget may be the easiest you will ever have to prepare. Indicate the purchase cost for the equipment, plus transportation and installation charges. Consider whether staff training to utilize the equipment properly and the added expenses of maintenance contracts should be included in your budget with the cost of its purchase.

9

Packaging the Proposal

Writing a well-articulated proposal represents the bulk of the work in preparing a solid proposal package. The remaining work is to package the document for the particular funder to whom it is being sent, based on your research and your contact with that funder to date (as described in Chapters 10 and 11).

Be sure to check the foundation's instructions for how and when to apply. Some foundations will accept proposals at any time. Others have specific deadlines. Foundations will also differ in the materials they want a grant applicant to submit. Some will list the specific information they want and the format you should adopt. Others will have an application form. In the course of the interviews for this book, it became apparent that an increasing number of foundations are developing an application form or a specific proposal format as a means of helping staff look at diverse information in a concise and consistent manner. Whatever the foundation's guidelines, pay careful attention to them and follow them.

Andrew Lark of the Frances L. and Edwin L. Cummings Memorial Fund makes this point: "It's amazing to see how many people get our guidelines and don't follow them."

In the following pages we will discuss the packaging of the document, including:

- cover letter or letter of transmittal;
- cover and title pages;
- table of contents; and
- appendix.

The Cover Letter

Often the cover letter is the basis for either consideration or rejection. Hildy Simmons of J. P. Morgan & Co., Incorporated states, "The cover letter is key. It should be clear and concise and make me want to turn the page. A few dos and don'ts:

- Do make a specific request. It's inconvenient if we have to dig for it.
- Do include a couple of paragraphs about why you are applying to us. But don't quote back to us our own contribution report.
- Do note references but don't name drop."

Julie Rogers of the Eugene and Agnes E. Meyer Foundation advises, "The cover letter is the best shot to make the proposal compelling. It should be humanizing."

What a waste for your agency's resources to invest time, energy, and money developing a proposal around a terrific project and then not have it read! To avoid this happening, be clear. Be succinct. And state immediately why the project fits within the funder's guidelines. For example, you might state, "Our funding research indicates that the XYZ Foundation has a special interest in the needs of children in foster care, which is the focus of this proposal." If the proposal does not fit the foundation's guidelines, this should be acknowledged immediately in the cover letter. You will then need to provide an explanation for why you are approaching this foundation.

If you had a conversation with someone in the funder's office prior to submitting the proposal, the cover letter should refer to it. For example, you might say, "I appreciate the time Jane Doe of your staff took to speak with me on December 1 about the Foundation." But do *not* imply that a proposal was requested if in fact it was not.

Sometimes in a discussion with a funder you will be told, "I can't encourage you to submit because. . . . However, if you want, you can go ahead and submit anyway." In this case, you should still refer to the conversation but your letter should demonstrate that you heard what the funder said. Andrew Lark of the Frances L. & Edwin L. Cummings Memorial Fund encourages grantseekers to call *after* they have carefully read the Fund's guidelines, but he wants subsequent correspondence to accurately reflect that conversation: "If we have had past contact or if we have ever funded you, remind us of that. But be careful how the letter reflects a prior conversation—avoid exaggeration."

The cover letter should also indicate what the reader will find in the proposal package. For example: "You will find enclosed two documents for your review. The first is a concise description of our project. The second is an appendix with the documents required by the Foundation for further review of our request."

Cite the name of the project, a precis of what it will accomplish, and the dollar amount of the request. For example: "Our After School Recreational Program will meet the educational and recreational needs of 50 disadvantaged Harlem children. We are seeking a grant of $25,000 from the Foundation to launch this project."

In the concluding paragraph of the cover letter, you should request a meeting with the funder. This can take place at the funder's office or on site at your agency. Also indicate your willingness to answer any questions that might arise or to provide additional information as required by the funder.

In summary, the cover letter should:

- indicate the size of the request;
- state why you are approaching this funder;
- mention any prior discussion of the proposal;
- describe the contents of the proposal package;

- briefly explain the project; and
- offer to set up a meeting and to provide additional information.

Who should sign the letter? Either the chairman of the board or the chief executive officer of your agency should be the spokesperson for all proposal submissions. Some funders insist on signature by the chairman of the board, indicating that the proposal has the support and endorsement of the board. However, signature by the executive director may allow for a sense of continuity that a rotating board chair cannot provide. If your group has no full-time staff, then the issue is resolved for you, and the board chairman should sign all requests. This would hold true also if your agency is in the process of searching for a new chief executive.

The proposal cover letter should never be signed by a member of the development staff. These individuals do the research, develop the proposals, and communicate with the funder, but generally they stay in the background when it comes to the submission of the proposal and any meetings with the funder. The individual who signs the cover letter should be the same person who signs subsequent correspondence, so that the organization has one spokesperson.

Variations may occur under special circumstances. For example, if a board member other than the chairperson is directly soliciting a peer, the cover letter should come from him or her. Alternatives would be for the letter to be signed by the chairman of the board and then for the board member to write a personal note on the original letter, or to send along a separate letter endorsing the proposal.

Following is a cover letter to the General Mills Foundation from WomenVenture. Note that the letter includes:

- reference to a prior conversation;
- the request;
- information about the project and the organization;
- some examples; and
- a promise to supply additional information, if needed.

Suzanne Fuller-Terrill
Associate Director and Senior Program Officer
General Mills Foundation
P.O. Box 1113
Minneapolis, MN 55440

Dear Suzanne:

Thank you for taking the time to meet with me last week. I appreciated having the opportunity to talk with you about WomenVenture and to learn about the current directions of the General Mills Foundation. As we discussed, I am writing to request that the General Mills Foundation continue its generous support with a 1996 general operating grant of $30,000. The purpose of this grant is to support the delivery of WomenVenture's services that help women to find jobs, plan careers and start and grow businesses, allowing them to earn *livable wages,* transition off public assistance and ultimately provide a better quality of life for themselves and their families.

WomenVenture continues to provide services for women of all social and economic backgrounds. The agency has, however, established a priority to build and maintain a diverse client profile while offering services that specifically address barriers that cause long-term dependency on public assistance. In 1995, WomenVenture made great progress toward reaching these objectives. Our year-end statistics show that 26.1% of clients served in 1995 were people of color and 40% of clients served had household incomes of less than $20,000.

Over the years, WomenVenture has seen many successes. Most recently, the overwhelming success of the agency's programs has lead to exciting expansion opportunities. In 1995, WomenVenture's Career Development Services developed a new job placement program that targets women who depend on public assistance, have a GED or high school-level education and little formal work experience. Through this program, participants are trained and placed in predetermined job opportunities identified through partnerships with corporate employers. WomenVenture's Initiatives in Non-Traditional Occupations also expanded in 1995 by launching its new comprehensive program that equips participants with the knowledge necessary for entry level employment in the printing industry. Finally, WomenVenture's Business Development Services has expanded its SETO program to serve refugee populations, beginning with the Hmong community.

The goal of this program is to support refugee entrepreneurs interested in starting or growing a business.

With the success and expansion of WomenVenture's programs comes numerous success stories about the individuals served through the agency's programs. For example:

- One client who completed WomenVenture's SETO program was able to start a successful business as an antiques dealer. The income from this business has allowed the family to transition off public assistance, become economically self-sufficient and they are now in the process of expanding their business to include a second location.

- To date, of the twelve women who graduated from the printing industry program's first pilot session on November 17, 1995, two participants have been placed in full-time jobs, three women were placed in temporary part-time work and three participants have enrolled in continued education—all in the printing industry.

- Another woman, who was unemployed when she came to WomenVenture's Career Development Services, was able to secure a job that included an annual salary of $31,000, tuition reimbursement to finish her four-year college degree and a promise of career advancement.

WomenVenture's comprehensive assessment process which will be introduced in 1996 and key program components help to ensure long-term success for the women we serve. These components include personal empowerment training that is unique to WomenVenture, specific business or employment training that incorporates hands-on experience, panel discussions and instruction from industry experts, and individualized consulting, business lending, placement and retention services.

Through its services, WomenVenture helps low-income women to achieve economic self-sufficiency. With this in mind, we ask the General Mills Foundation to continue its support in 1996. If you have any questions about our programs or the enclosed materials, please call me at 646-3808. Thank you for your serious consideration of this request.

Sincerely,

Kay Gudmestad
President

Here is another example of a cover letter, this one from Project Reach Youth. It has the following characteristics:

- It is very brief.
- It refers to past contact and funding.
- It requests specific support.

Ms. Roberta Ruocco
Vice President
Community Relations and Public Affairs
J. P. Morgan & Co., Inc.
60 Wall Street
46th Floor
New York, New York 10260-0060

Dear Roberta,

It was good to talk with you last week. We have had a very active summer and are gearing up for the fall.

Enclosed is our proposal for general support for Project Reach Youth. We are requesting $20,000 per year for two years in order to continue to implement and enrich our new programs and services.

We are so very grateful to J. P. Morgan for the terrific support you have provided, and we look to J. P. Morgan to help us continue to provide innovative programs and unique services to enable the children to reach their full potential.

Yours truly,

Janet Kelley
Executive Director

A final example is from the YWCA of Plainfield/North Plainfield, New Jersey. It was well received by the grantmaker who was familiar with the applying organization. Sometimes candor—mixed with a touch of humor—can be very effective.

Mr. Robert Parsons, Jr.
Chairman
Charles E. & Joy C. Pettinos Foundation
437 Southern Boulevard
Chatham Township, NJ 07928

Dear Mr. Parsons:

I know, I know that my proposal is being submitted to you after March 1st. This is completely my fault, and I will understand if the foundation's managers determine that our request is ineligible for consideration at this time.

We have just entered into a new phase of the Campaign, and I have taken on a number of new responsibilities—and one of them was to submit this proposal. But I just didn't get up to speed in time.

If you are able to consider support for the YWCA, we will all be grateful. This is a big project for us, but it is going very well and we have experienced such kindness and generosity from so many in the past year.

> Mr. Parsons, I appreciate your past support. If you are not able to accept this proposal now, I hope I will have the opportunity to resubmit at another time. But please don't report me to my Board!
>   Thank you again.
>
> Sincerely,
>
> Jacquelyn M. Glock, MSW
> Executive Director

Cover Page and Title

The cover page has three functions:

1. to convey specific information to the reader;
2. to protect the proposal; and
3. to reflect the professionalism of the preparer.

You should personalize the information on the cover page by including the name of the funder. You might present the information as follows:

> A PROPOSAL TO THE XYZ FOUNDATION

or

> A REQUEST DEVELOPED FOR THE XYZ FOUNDATION

Then note the title of the project:

A CAMPAIGN FOR STABILITY

Provide key information that the funder might need to contact your agency:

Submitted by:
Mary Smith
Executive Director
The Nonprofit Organization
40 Canal Street
New York, NY 10013
212-935-5300

It is possible that your cover letter will be separated from the rest of the proposal. Without key information on the cover page, the funder could fail to follow up with your agency.

The cover page from WomenVenture's proposal to the General Mills Foundation serves as an example.

**A Request to the General Mills Foundation for a
1996 grant of $30,000 to support
WomenVenture's Comprehensive Services**

Submitted by

WomenVenture
2324 University Avenue
St. Paul, MN 55114
646-3808

Kay Gudmestad
President

The title you assign to your proposal can have a surprisingly significant impact on the reader. It should reflect what your project is all about. "A CAMPAIGN FOR STABILITY" tells the reader that there is a formal effort taking place and that the result will be to bring stability to the nonprofit applicant. It is short and to the point, while being descriptive.

There are a few suggestions for developing the title for a proposal:

- Don't try to be cute. Fundraising is a serious matter. A cute title implies that the proposal is not a serious attempt to solve a real problem.

- Do not duplicate the title of another project in your agency or one of another nonprofit that might be well known to the funder. It can cause confusion.

- Be sure the title means something. If it is just words, try again, or don't use any title at all.

Coming up with the title can be a tricky part of proposal writing. If you are stuck, try these suggestions:

- Seek the advice of the executive director, the project director, or a creative person in the organization or outside.

- Hold an informal competition for staff or volunteers to see who can come up with the best title.

- Go to the board with a few ideas and ask board members to select the one that makes the most sense.

- Jot down a list of key words from the proposal. Add a verb or two and experiment with the word order.

Let's take a look at a few actual titles and evaluate their effectiveness.

Title	Effectiveness
Forward Face	Arouses interest but does not tell you anything about the project.
	This is a proposal that seeks funds for facial reconstruction for disfigured children. With the help of the nonprofit group involved, the children will have a new image with which to face the future. The title is a pun, which is cute but not very effective.
Vocational, Educational Employment Project	This title tells us that three types of services will be offered.
	The project serves disadvantaged youth, which is not mentioned. The effectiveness of this title could be improved if the population served were somehow alluded to.
Building a Healthier Tomorrow	This title implies that construction will occur, and indeed it is the title for a capital campaign. It also suggests that the construction is for some kind of health facility.
	This proposal is for a YMCA to improve its health-wellness facilities. Thus, the title is very effective in conveying the purpose of the proposal.

You should evaluate any titles you come up with by anticipating the reaction of the uninitiated funding representative who will be reading this proposal.

Table of Contents

Simply put, the table of contents tells the reader what information will be found in the proposal. The various sections should be listed in the order in which they appear, with page numbers indicating where in the document they can be located. The table should be laid out in such a way that it takes up one full page.

Following the proposal format we have recommended, a table of contents would look like this:

TABLE OF CONTENTS	Page
Executive Summary	1
Statement of Need	2
Project Description	4
Budget	7
Organization Information	9
Conclusion	10

By stating where to find specific pieces of information, you are being considerate of the proposal reader, who might want an overview of what information is included and might also want to be selective in the initial review.

A sample follows. It is from a proposal for the East Side House Settlement.

Table of Contents

1) Executive Summary	
2) Program Narrative	
The Need	1
The Response	2
Project READY Goals and Objectives	2
Staff and Participants	3
The Program	3
a) College Resource Center	3
b) The Comprehensive Internship	4
c) Career and Educational Development Workshops	4
d) College Mentors	5
e) College Options	5
f) Evaluation	5
3) Program Budget	7
Appendices	

The Appendix

The appendix is a reference tool for the funder. Include in it any information not included elsewhere that the foundation or corporate grantmaker indicates is required for review of your request. Not every proposal requires one.

The appendix should be stapled together separately from the proposal narrative. Because it usually contains information that the funder has specifically requested, keeping it separate makes it easy for the funder to find. The appendix may have its own table of contents indicating to the reader what follows and where to find it.

A sample table of contents to a proposal appendix, taken from the WomenVenture proposal, follows:

Attachments

1. 1996 Operating Budget
2. WomenVenture's Board of Directors
3. IRS Tax Exemption Letter
4. 1994 Audited Financial Statements
5. Selected Press Clippings
6. List of Major Contributors
7. 1994 Annual Report

You may wish to include any or all of the following items in the appendix:

1. A board list. This should contain the name of each board member and that person's business or other affiliation. Adding further contact information such as address and telephone number is optional. The reader will use this to identify people he or she knows or whose names are familiar.

    An excerpt from the board list for WomenVenture serves as an example:

WomenVenture Board of Directors

Board Officers

Christine A. Morrison, Chair
Community Volunteer

Marialice Harwood, First Vice Chair
Regional Account Marketing
   Executive
ADVO, Inc.

Randi S. N. Yoder, Vice Chair
Associate Dean of External Affairs
Carlson School of Management, U of M

Ezell Jones, Secretary
President & CEO
Premier RiskTech Services

Kathy McKinstry, Treasurer
Community Volunteer

Directors

Albert Alexander
President
Ridgedale First Bank

Nancy Zalusky Berg
Attorney
Walling & Berg

Lois B. Bishop
Community Volunteer

Linda Donaldson
President
Brighton Development Corporation

Marvin Granath
Attorney
Granath and O'Donnell, P.A.

Kay Gudmestad
President
WomenVenture

Lucy B. Hartwell
Community Volunteer

Gayle L. Holmes
President
Menttium Corporation (MN 100)

Orlena A. Iverson
Vice President, Commercial
   Department
TCF Bank

Kathleen A. Knutson
Law Clerk
Musicland

Joan C. McBride
Director, Sales & Marketing Services
3M

Annette Minor
Vice President & Assistant Director
   of Compliance
Piper Jaffray Inc.

Mickey Mulcahy
Vice President, Organization
   Development
St. Paul Companies

Marcia Murray
Quality Specialist
U S WEST Communications

Jeanette M. Rupert
District Manager
ATI Title Company

Nancy Sinsabaugh
Vice President
EduServ Technologies

2. Your nonprofit's IRS Letter of Determination. This document, issued by the IRS, indicates that your agency has been granted 501(c)(3) status and is "not a private foundation." Gifts made to your organization are deductible for tax purposes. This letter is often requested by funders. Foundations can give most easily to publicly supported organizations, and corporations want their gifts to be tax deductible. If your organization is religiously affiliated or a government entity, you might not have such a letter, and you should explain that fact to the funder.

3. Financial information. The operating budget for the current fiscal year, and the latest audited financial statement are often appropriate to include. Some funders request your latest 990 in order to assess the financial stability of your organization. If your agency is religiously affiliated, or for some other reason you do not file a 990, you will need to explain this fact to a funder that requests it. You may want to include a list of donors for the past fiscal year by name and size of gift. Grantmakers want to know which foundations and corporations are being approached to help with the project under review. Add that information, as well. An excerpt from the WomenVenture support list follows.

WomenVenture

Major Corporate and Foundation Contributors
1995 and 1996 over $1,000

Contributor	1995	1996	
ADC Telecommunications	$ 2,000	$ 3,000	to be submitted
American Express	10,000	10,000	to be submitted
American National Bank	1,000	1,000	to be submitted
Elmer and Eleanor Andersen Foundation	1,500	1,500	to be submitted
Hugh J. Andersen Foundation	5,500	5,500	to be submitted
David Winton Bell Foundation	3,000	5,000	pending
James Ford Bell Foundation—Project	20,000	15,000	pending
Bemis Company Foundation—General	5,000	5,500	to be submitted
Best Buy Companies, Inc.—Project	2,000	2,000	to be submitted
F. R. Bigelow Foundation—Project	25,000	10,000	to be submitted
Bush Foundation—Project	90,000	45,000	committed
Byerly's	1,500	1,500	to be submitted
CP Rail Systems	3,000	3,500	to be submitted
Cargill	6,000	6,000	to be submitted
Ceredian	1,000	1,000	to be submitted
Cherne Foundation—Project		5,000	to be submitted
Dain Bosworth Foundation	2,000	2,000	to be submitted
Dayton Hudson Foundation	60,000	60,000	to be submitted
Donaldson Foundation	2,000	2,000	to be submitted
Ecolab, Inc.	2,500	3,000	pending
Elizabeth C. Quinlan Foundation	1,000	1,000	to be submitted
Fingerhut Corporation	750	1,000	committed
First Bank System Foundation	25,000	25,000	to be submitted
General Mills Foundation—General	30,000	30,000	to be submitted

4. Résumés of key staff. If the background information on key staff members is not included as part of the project statement of the proposal, it should be included in the appendix. This also might be the place to include the organization chart, if you feel it would be helpful.

Do not include in the appendix anything that is not required by the funder or deemed essential to making your case. The key is to give the funder what is needed for review of your proposal without making the package look overwhelming. For example, many nonprofits like to add press clippings to the appendix. If they make the package appear unnecessarily bulky and are tangential to the grant review, they should be sent to the funder at another time when they will receive more attention. However, should these clippings be essential to the review of the request, then by all means include them.

At this stage of assembling the proposal, you have a cover letter and two additional separately packaged components: the proposal narrative and the appendix. If each is clearly identifiable, you will save the funder time and energy in the initial review of your proposal.

Packaging

Packaging refers to both the physical preparation of the documents and their assembly.

Physical Preparation

Every proposal package should be individually prepared for each funder. This permits you to customize the submission in order to reflect the interests of a specific funder and to show them that you've done your homework. This is the point at which you need to double-check the guidelines for a funder's specific requirements for the proposal package.

If you are using word-processing equipment, it will be relatively easy to customize the cover letter, title page, and other components of the package that have variables in them. For those components that are photocopied, be sure that the originals you are working from are crisp and legible. For example, if your IRS Letter of Determination is in poor condition, write to the Internal Revenue Service at the key district IRS office in your region, Exempt Organizations Division, and ask for a fresh copy of the letter. The request must be on your organization's official letterhead. The letter should contain your organization's name, address, taxpayer ID number, and a daytime telephone number, and it must be signed by an officer with that person's title. For the other documents, copy from originals whenever possible.

Assembly

When a proposal arrives in a funder's office, any binding is usually removed before the proposal is reviewed. Therefore, do not waste money on binding for the proposal and the appendix. Simply staple each document, or use a plastic strip to hold together each document.

You have three documents: the cover letter, the proposal, and the appendix. The latter two are separately stapled. In all likelihood, these documents will require a manila envelope. Be certain that the addressee and return address information are printed clearly on the envelope. You might want to put a piece of cardboard in the envelope to protect the documents. Then insert the three documents with the cover letter on top, followed by the proposal and the appendix.

With regard to the funder's address, if you are following the procedure recommended in Chapter 11 for submitting this request, you will have had a conversation with the funder's office prior to submitting the proposal. Use that opportunity to verify the address and the name of the person to whom the package is to be sent.

10

Researching Potential Funders

Once you have drafted your proposal, you are ready to develop your prospect list of foundations and/or corporations that might be interested in funding it. What you learn during this process will help you prepare different proposal packages, as described in Chapter 9, depending on the specific funder information you uncover.

The foundation and corporate executives interviewed for this book repeatedly advised grantseekers to pay special attention to the research effort. Most felt that sufficient information is available to enable nonprofit organizations to do their homework, thereby obtaining a clear picture of the interests of potential funders.

There are three steps you should follow in your research:

- Compile
- Investigate
- Refine

Compile

Compile a list of foundations, corporations, and other funders whose geographic and/or program interests might lead them to support your agency and the specific projects for which you are seeking funding. Try to be inclusive at this stage. If you think a specific foundation or corporate donor should be on the list, go ahead and include them. Let further research on the source tell you otherwise.

At the compilation stage, you have a variety of resources to draw upon in addition to the standard funding directories. Check your local newspaper for articles about corporations or businesses in your area. Talk to your local chamber of commerce and civic groups such as the Rotary and Lions Club. Be resourceful as you compile your list of possible funders.

You will also want to be aware of who is funding other agencies in your community. These foundations and corporations may be likely sources of support for your own agency. This information can be difficult to unearth. Sometimes another local agency's annual report will list its funders; nonprofits occasionally will publicly thank their funders in the local newspaper; arts organizations usually will list their donors in programs. The grants database in *FC Search: The Foundation Center's Database on CD-ROM* and the Foundation Center's publications *The Foundation Grants Index* and *Who Gets Grants* contain the names of recipients of grants from 1,000 of the largest foundations and those that report directly to the Center.

Investigate

Next, take your list and investigate each source. There are definitive resources available to you to research foundations. The IRS requires foundations to file an annual 990-PF form reporting on assets and grants. You will base your research on directories that have been compiled using the 990-PF or from information provided directly to the directory publisher, on materials published by the foundations themselves or on the 990-PF itself. It is more difficult to obtain information on corporate giving. Corporations may use two grantmaking vehicles: a private foundation and a corporate giving program. If a corporation has a foundation, then a 990-PF will be filed just as with other private foundations. If the corporation has a separate giving program, it is not required to file a publicly available report on gifts made under this program. Some corporations do issue special reports on their philanthropic endeavors, and a number of directories devoted specifically to corporate giving are published regularly.

Here is what you are looking for in any of the resources you use:

- A track record of giving in your geographic locale, in your field of interest, or for the type of support you seek, be it basic operating support or funding for construction or equipment.

- Grants of a size compatible with your agency's needs. (Bear in mind that in all likelihood your project will have more than one funder.)

- Funders that have not already committed their resources many years into the future and that do not appear simply to fund the same nonprofit groups year in and year out.

Print and Electronic Directories

Appendix D contains a list of print and electronic publications you can utilize in your investigation effort. The Foundation Center is the preeminent source of information on foundation and corporate funders. *FC Search: The Foundation Center's Database on CD-ROM*, the Center's print directories, and many other resources are made available to the public at its libraries and cooperating collections in sites all around the country. The Center's collections also usually·include copies of foundation guidelines, annual reports, and even newspaper clippings on local or national foundations. Where detailed database or annual report information is lacking, you can examine copies of a foundation's 990-PF at one of the Foundation Center's library collections. Call toll free 1-800-424-9836 to learn of the library collection nearest you.

Print and CD-ROM directories will most likely be your primary resource in investigating the foundations on your list. But you must not stop there. Often you will find additional or more up-to-date information in other resources.

The Internet

Grantseekers are beginning to discover a wealth of information on the Internet. Although locating that information can be daunting at first, there are many helpful resources on the subject. The Foundation Center maintains its own World Wide Web site on the Internet, http://fdncenter.org. The Center's Web site is an easy-to-use gateway to a wide range of philanthropic information resources. Visitors to the Center's Web site can also readily access many other Internet sites, including those maintained by private, corporate, and community foundations; nonprofit organizations; government agencies; and other groups that provide information of interest to nonprofit organizations.

The Internet is in a constant state of flux. You might want to get in the habit of "surfing the Net" to keep abreast of its continually expanding resources. Because there is no editorial oversight of the information available on the Internet, you must evaluate the accuracy and scope of that information yourself. For these and other reasons, it is a good idea to use the Internet as a supplement to traditional research methods.

Guidelines

Many of the larger foundations, as well as community foundations, issue guidelines, sometimes in pamphlet form but often as a section of their annual report. Foundation trustees and staff generally care deeply about the problems in society and struggle to determine the most effective strategies they can use to produce the greatest impact with their funding dollars. When they issue guidelines or announce areas of programmatic interests, these are the result of careful planning and strategy. You should thoroughly review any available guidelines as part of your investigation of a foundation or corporate donor. Some guidelines are very specific, stating goals or even projects to be funded within each area of interest. Others are more general and require further investigation.

If the foundation in question supports only medical research in Kenya, and your agency provides after-school reading programs for children in Columbus, Ohio, this is not a good prospect and should probably not be on your list. However, if you are doing medical research at Stanford University that has implications for the population in Africa, there is a chance that the foundation might be interested in your work, if not now, then perhaps in the future.

Don't assume that a funder's guidelines from two years ago are still applicable today, particularly when a funder's assets are growing rapidly or it is experiencing a change in leadership. While the foundation probably will not shift its area of interest overnight from the arts to medicine, there may well be subtle changes in emphasis. You need to be aware of these before making your request. Jessica Chao, former vice president of the DeWitt Wallace–Reader's Digest Fund, notes, "We get so many proposals where it is clear they are looking at our guidelines from three years ago. They obviously haven't made the effort to learn about our current interests."

The Annual Report

A foundation's annual report may prove to be your most valuable tool in researching a funder. It is important not only for determining current giving patterns but also for projecting future trends. The annual report reflects the personality, style, and interests of the foundation.

In reading an annual report, you should look most closely at two sections. First, read the statement by the chairman, president, or chief executive. Look for clues that reveal the foundation's philosophical objectives. What are the problems in society that the foundation wants to address? What kind of impact do they hope to make with the foundation's funds? This section will also reveal if the foundation is in the process of changing directions. Such a shift presents you with a significant window of opportunity, if your project happens to fit within new areas they want to explore.

The other section to examine is the list of grantees for the past year. Check the grants list against what the foundation *says* it wants to fund. You are looking for clues that will illustrate their specific interests. You also want to look for any discrepancies. Do they say, for instance, that they don't fund capital campaigns, yet right there listed under the grants is a donation of $75,000 to the St. Clairesville Community Center to build a new gymnasium? This doesn't necessarily mean that you should keep them on your prospect list for your own gymnasium. It does mean that you should research the foundation further. Many foundations fund projects or agencies with special connections to the foundation or in which their trustees have a particular interest even though they fall outside their stated guidelines.

The 990-PF will not give you as much information about a foundation as guidelines or an annual report will, but if those are lacking, it is the place you can turn to find a foundation's grants list.

Refine

With information in hand about each foundation or corporation on your original list, you should refine your prospect list. Take care at this stage to focus only on those sources that are *most likely* to help your nonprofit now or in the future. Then ask yourself:

- Have I developed a thorough, well-rounded prospect list?
- Is it manageable? Given the need and the time I have to devote to fundraising, is the list too long or too short?

As you winnow your list, one question will arise: Does my project need to fit precisely within a funder's stated guidelines? Guidelines often indicate a particular area of interest, but they should not be viewed as definitive restrictions. A funder may be looking into changing its areas of support precisely at the time your proposal arrives; or someone at the foundation might evince some special interest in your project. Each foundation or corporate funder is unique and responds accordingly. Use your common sense when determining whether it is too much of a stretch to go to the next step in exploring a particular funder.

11

Contacting and Cultivating Potential Funders

Making the Initial Contact

Once you have determined that a foundation is a likely funder, then you must initiate the contact. Some foundations prefer that you call first to see if your project fits their specific guidelines. Be aware, however, that this is not a popular step with all funders. The reality is that the majority of foundations don't have staff to answer the telephones, and those that do are usually overwhelmed with calls and paper work. One funder interviewed for this book adamantly stated, "I hate telephone calls!"

If you do decide to call first, be sure you don't appear to be going on a fishing expedition. Funders find this particularly annoying. Your conversation needs to make it clear that you have read their guidelines and want further clarification on whether your particular project would fit. You are *not* making a solicitation by telephone.

Funders caution that, if you do call, listen carefully to what is being said. Ilene Mack of the William Randolph Hearst Foundation commented, "I am happy to have a conversation with a grantseeker. This way I can understand what kind of organization they are and if we are an appropriate fit."

On the other hand, both Ilene Mack and Jane Quinn of the DeWitt Wallace–Reader's Digest Fund also caution the grantseeker to be careful to "listen for the 'no.' "

There are three objectives to the initial call:

- It promotes name recognition of your group.
- It tests the possible compatibility between the potential funder and your agency.
- It permits you to gather additional information about the funder and about possible reaction to your project *before* you actually submit your proposal.

How should you proceed? First, rehearse what you will say about your organization. You may be given just a few minutes by the foundation or corporate representative. Also, have on hand the background information you have compiled about the potential funder and how much and what you would like them to fund. If there is a prior relationship with your nonprofit group, be aware of the details.

Second, make the call. It would be great if you could speak directly with the president of the foundation or senior vice president in charge of corporate contributions. But this will not often happen. Be satisfied with anyone who can respond to your questions. In the process, don't underestimate the importance of support staff. They can be very helpful. They can provide you with key information and ensure that your proposal is processed promptly. Be sure to obtain the name of the person you do speak with so that reference to this conversation can be made when you submit your formal request. This may be your contact person for future calls and letters.

What should you say? Be prepared to:

- Introduce your agency: give the name, location, purpose, and goals.
- State up front why you are calling: you want to learn more about this funder with the ultimate purpose of obtaining financial support.

- Inquire if you can submit a proposal: be specific about which one and the hoped-for level of support.
- Request an appointment: few funders are willing to grant the request for a meeting without at least an initial proposal on the table, but it's always worth checking. As a matter of fact, each time you speak with a funder, you should inquire if a face-to-face conversation would be appropriate.

Variations will emerge in each call, so you must be sharp, alert, and ready to respond to the funder. At the same time, try to seem relaxed and confident as the discussion proceeds. Remember that you are a potential partner for the prospective funder.

Many foundations have no staff or limited office support. Some corporations assign their philanthropic activities to executives with very heavy workloads. The point is, repeated calls may go unanswered. Above all, be persistent. Persistence will set your agency apart from many nonprofits whose leaders initiate fundraising with determination but quickly lose heart. If you cannot get through to a potential funder on the telephone, send a letter of inquiry designed to gain the same information as the call. If your letter goes unanswered, then be prepared to submit a request anyway.

While some program officers do not like to meet before a proposal is submitted, others say that they would prefer the proposal to be submitted *after* a meeting.

The message here is that, like people, every foundation is different. Foundations, in fact, are made up of people. It is important to listen to, and to respect, what the funding representative is telling you.

Submitting the Proposal

Actually submitting the proposal may seem anticlimactic considering the amount of preparation that has gone into identifying and researching the prospective funders and putting together the various components. But once you have determined that a meeting prior to submission is not possible or is unnecessary, or once you've had the desired meeting, eventually there comes the time to submit the full proposal to the funders on your list.

Checklists may prove useful at this point. You may wish to check and double-check one last time to ensure that all requirements of the funder have been met and that all of the pieces of the proposal package are there in the proper sequence. Above all, you will want to be sure that you submit the proposal in accordance with the funder's deadline. If possible, send in your proposal at least two weeks in advance of the deadline. This enables the funder to request additional information, if needed.

Grantseekers often wonder whether they should mail in their proposals, send by overnight mail or messenger, or hand-deliver them. By far the best choice is the least expensive one. Use regular mail unless there is a very good reason to do otherwise.

Cultivating the Potential Funder

Don't forget to continue to communicate once you have submitted your proposal. Cultivation of the funding prospect can make the critical difference between getting a grant and getting lost in the shuffle.

Knowledge of the funder's situation, and of that particular grantmaker's procedures for processing proposals, can be extremely helpful in developing your cultivation strategy.

Funders are flooded with proposals. Even if they turn down all that are clearly outside their guidelines, they still get many more than their budgets will allow them to fund. Hunter Corbin of the Hyde and Watson Foundation indicated, "We get 800–900 appeals a year. Seventy-five to 80 percent would qualify for support." And John Marshall of the Kresge Foundation noted, "One-half of our grantees each year have not been funded by us before."

How can you assure that your proposal will be one of those to get into the grant pipeline? The ways in which foundations operate differ widely. At some small family foundations, the donor himself or herself will review all requests. At the larger foundations, a first cut is usually made to eliminate those that are out of program, then program officers review proposals in specific areas and must take a proposal through a staff review process before a recommendation goes to their board of trustees. Andrew Lark describes the Frances L. & Edwin L. Cummings Memorial Fund's process: "There is an immediate rejection if a request is out of our ballpark. We generally ask those being considered to fill out a Cummings Fund questionnaire form. Then we do site visits. We look for efficiency in the way they run the program, realism in the application, and strong board/management involvement."

Foundations frequently work closely with the grantseeker in developing the request. As John Cook of the Henry Luce Foundation points out, "A staff person will aid the grantseeker in proposal design." Susan Lajoie of the Cleveland Foundation notes: "A program officer will follow up, offering guidance regarding the proposal submission."

At the DeWitt Wallace–Reader's Digest Fund, Jane Quinn describes the review process as follows: "The key to working with us is to do your homework and play by the rules. First you have to find a fit with our mission. Next, submit a one- to two-page query letter, as noted in our annual report. There will be a response within eight weeks. If there is a possibility of a fit, we will meet and ask for more data. The proposal is submitted pretty far into the process. We view it as the plan against which to measure effectiveness."

John Marshall of the Kresge Foundation summarizes the challenge facing nonprofit agencies: "Agencies have to make informed choices about the sources to which they will apply. Then they need to follow that up with good communication and a carefully constructed application. Speed doesn't take the place of judgment."

Several forms of cultivation may be particularly valuable after the proposal is submitted:

- Communication by phone,
- Face-to-face meetings,
- Using board contacts, and
- Written updates and progress reports.

Communication by Phone

Normally you should plan to call about two weeks after the proposal package is mailed. The primary purpose of this call is to make sure that the proposal has been received. You have requested a meeting in the cover letter and offered to supply any additional information required to help the funder consider your request. You should therefore ask if it is appropriate to schedule a meeting at the foundation or corporate office or a site visit at your agency. Be sure to ask about the process and timing for the review of your proposal. This will guide you as to when you might call back or send updated information.

Call periodically thereafter to check on the status of your proposal. If you have had no response in the expected time frame, call to find out if there has been a change in the schedule. Ask the same types of questions as you did previously: Is additional information required? When will the proposal be reviewed? Would the foundation or corporate representative like to meet? Be brief. There is a fine line between being helpful and being too pushy.

Each time you call, be prepared to answer the program officer's detailed questions about any aspect of the proposal or of your agency's work. You should also expect to receive calls from your program officer during the course of the proposal review.

Hunter Corbin of the Hyde and Watson Foundation warns the grantseeker that it frustrates the funder "when you call the nonprofit, and no one knows what the application is all about. Worse, you call the organization and request information, and no one calls you back."

It helps to stay in touch by phone. This gives you a chance to find out what is happening with your proposal and to share information with the foundation or corporate funder.

When appropriate, follow up the phone conversation with a note about the next step you plan to take or confirming any new information you provided over the phone. While phone communication is often the most convenient way to keep in touch, you need to be sure that any agreement or information that is critical to a successful outcome of the review process is put in writing.

Face-to-Face Meetings

Appointments can be very hard to obtain. Many funders will not agree to a meeting until the proposal is under active consideration. This might entail assigning it to a program officer, who would then be the person to meet with you. Even when the foundation or corporate representative respects your group or is intensely interested in your project, he or she may believe that a meeting would not be helpful in arriving at a recommendation on your request. However, some foundations insist on a site visit for most or all of the groups to which they make grants.

When you are offered an appointment, you should view this as a very special opportunity. It is one that you must prepare for carefully.

First, be sure that the right team is selected to attend the meeting. If your nonprofit agency has staff, the chief executive officer or executive director should go. The CEO should be able to answer specific questions relating to the project. The other member of the team should be a volunteer, preferably from the board. The presence of the volunteer underscores the fact that the board is aware of and supports the work of the organization. Under the right circumstances, a member of the program staff can be a helpful adjunct, or you must bring along someone who benefits from the good work of your organization. But don't overwhelm the funder by bringing too many additional people to the meeting. John Mason of the Monsanto Fund reported his dismay when the grantseeker "brings an army of folks to visit. Fifteen people fill up my conference room, and only one of them speaks." Clear with the funding representative precisely how many people plan to attend. If time permits, call a day in advance to confirm the date and remind the funder who is coming. A site visit obviously allows you to introduce the funding representative to a wider range of people involved in your agency or project.

Next, prepare for the meeting. Compile background information about the foundation or corporation. You should be careful to note any prior interaction with the funder, especially if it was less than positive. Develop a profile of the person(s) with whom you are meeting, if this information is available in standard biographical sources or via the grapevine. Your peers in the nonprofit world who are grant recipients might shed some light on the personality and idiosyncracies of the funder.

Create a role for each of the participants. It is critical that no one sits idle. There should be a dialogue and rapport among the meeting participants.

Last, know precisely what you want to accomplish in the meeting. You won't leave with a check in hand, but you do need to decide in advance what information you want to share and to obtain.

You should expect to accomplish a great deal through the simple process of meeting face to face with the funder. The meeting will establish a personal relationship between the representatives of your organization and of the funding agency. Despite our high-tech world, giving is still a highly personal activity. Hence, the better your rapport with the donor, the more likely it is that financial support will be forthcoming.

Along with getting to know the people at your agency, this will be an opportunity for the funding representative to gain a much better understanding of your group's work. Hearing from knowledgeable people about your mission, programs, and dreams will allow the funder to ask questions, to refine information, and to correct misperceptions.

Equally important, the funder will gain a much better sense of the project for which you are seeking support. Critical information about the proposal, such as the need, methods for addressing it, and the capability of your group to run the program, might be covered during discussion. For this reason, be sure to review the proposal carefully before the meeting.

You must assume responsibility for the agenda of the meeting. Be prepared to:

- Use an icebreaker. The first few times you attend a meeting with a funder, it can be nerve-racking. Break the tension by telling an amusing anecdote, by relaying a true incident of interest to the group, or by commenting about the view or an object in the room where the meeting takes place.

- Introduce all of the meeting participants. This way the funder will know the players and be clear to whom specific questions should be addressed.

- Get down to business. Once introduced, the participants should promptly move on to the real purpose of the meeting: your group hopes the funder will become a partner with you in getting your project off the ground.

- Remind the funder about the mission and history of your agency. Be thorough but brief in this review.

- Describe the programs you offer. Again, be succinct, but be certain that the funder has a good overview of your services. This is important in case the project submitted for funding proves not to be of interest. The funder may request a proposal relating to a different aspect of your agency's work, having achieved a good grasp of the whole program.

- Describe the project for which you are seeking support. It is critical that you demonstrate the conviction that success is likely. Provide the necessary detail for the funder to understand the problem being addressed and your agency's proposed response to it.

- Keep a dialogue going. It is easy to speak at length about your organization. But it is also easy to bore the funders and, even worse, for you to come away from the meeting not having gained any relevant new information about this grantmaker. Whenever possible, try to elicit the funder's reactions. Inquire about current programs they have funded that address similar problems. Treat the grantmaker as a potential partner. Remember, their dollars have significance only when combined with programs. Listen carefully to their responses, comments, and questions. This dialogue will clue you into the *real* interests and concerns of this potential funder. Don't assume anything.

- Obtain a clear understanding of the next steps. You should determine the following: if anything more is needed for review of the request; when the proposal will come up for review; and how the agency will be notified about the outcome. If, as a result of this conversation, it is clear that the proposal is unlikely to be funded, you should ask what you might do to resubmit this or another proposal.

A great deal can be accomplished in a well-crafted meeting, whether at their place or yours. You don't want this process spoiled by extending it for too long. Once it is clear that the objectives have been achieved, you need to summarize the next steps to be taken by both sides and move on to a cordial goodbye. End the meeting while the "good vibes" are still being felt by both sides.

Using Board Contacts

A contact from one of your board members with a peer affiliated with the foundation or corporate funder you are approaching will usually reinforce the relationship you are building.

How do you discover if your board members have contacts that can help with raising funds? First, circulate to all of the members of your board the names of the officers and directors of the foundations and corporations you plan to approach. Ask your board members to respond to you by a certain date about those whom they know. Then work one-on-one with individual board members, building a strategy for them to utilize their contacts. Another approach is to meet with the board members to talk about individuals with whom they can be helpful. You may find contacts with funders that you had not intended to approach, where having an entree will make a difference.

Knowing that you have board-to-board contact is not enough. You must assist your board member in capitalizing on this relationship on behalf of your nonprofit group. First, develop a scenario with the board member focusing on how to approach the contact. The more personal the approach, the better it is. Second, assist your board member with understanding why this funder would want to help your organization, finding the right language to discuss your agency and your funding needs, and drafting correspondence as needed. Then make sure that the board member makes the promised contact. Periodically remind this individual of the next step to be taken. The groundwork you have done is wasted if the board member never follows through.

Be forewarned that staff of foundations and corporate grantmakers may be concerned about your board members contacting their board members. This is particularly true of professionally staffed foundations where program officers may consider it inappropriate or may view it as interference. Some funders feel strongly that an agency should not use a board contact, even if they have one.

Still others report that their trustees are encouraged to indicate their interest in a project. At a minimum, staff want to know in advance that a board contact will be used.

Where you already are in contact with the foundation staff, it is critical to discuss a board contact with them before it is set in motion. Finally, keep in mind that relying on board contacts can backfire. At some foundations if a board member has had contact with an agency, he or she is expected to disqualify himself from discussion about the specific proposal.

Written Updates and Progress Reports

Written communication helps a foundation or corporate donor learn more about your group and reminds them that you need their support. You should plan to send materials selectively while your proposal is under review. Here are some ideas for what you might send:

- summary reports on what is going on in your organization;

- financial information, such as a new audit;

- newsletters, bulletins, brochures, or other frequently issued information;

- updates/reports on specific projects; and

- newspaper or magazine articles on the project for which you have requested support, the work of your nonprofit, or closely related issues.

It is usually not necessary to customize the materials, but a brief accompanying note always helps to reinforce your relationship with the funder.

Here are two examples of update letters:

Ms. Elizabeth Costas
Administrative Director
The Frances L. & Edwin L. Cummings Memorial Fund
501 Fifth Avenue, Suite 708
New York, NY 10017-6103

Dear Libby:

I was delighted to have the opportunity to discuss with you, Andy and Grace the progress that Teach For America has made over the past several months. By all accounts, the organization has measurably matured and is now squarely on the road to becoming a stable, ongoing institution. The reconstruction of our board of directors, the appointment of a new chairperson and the formation of local community advisory boards have been pivotal steps in this regard. These actions have enabled us to attract new leadership and financial support to the organization. A list of our national board is enclosed for your information. As I noted earlier, we are presently in the process of adding more fundraising heft to this group.

Sue Lehmann, our new board chair, brings valuable experience in the education arena, as a volunteer and professionally, in addition to bringing a wealth of new contacts nationwide to the organization. One of Sue's areas of interest is teacher education which is reflected in the formation of our Professional Advisory Council. Sue is also on the boards of the Fund for New York City Public Education, the New Visions Advisory Board and the Corporation For National Service. She also serves as a consultant to several foundations in the field of education, including the MacArthur Foundation, the Rockefeller Foundation and the Surdna Foundation. Sue also was an advisor to former New York City Schools Chancellors Joseph Fernandez and Raymond Cortines.

Our Professional Advisory Council is one of several components of a revamped approach to providing our corps members with the assistance they need to be most effective in the classroom. As I mentioned during our meeting, each of our regions is now also establishing partnerships with local universities and schools of education to facilitate our corps members' professional development. While we are still not yet where we would like to be in this regard, we are very pleased that our corps members receive high marks from the people who have the most direct experience working with them, school principals. I have enclosed the complete report of the survey of school principals and superintendents conducted by Kane, Parsons and Associates which I referred to in our meeting.

I would also like to thank you, Andy and Grace for the many suggestions offered during our meeting. We know that we need many partners in the development process and appreciate your suggestions and interest. I spoke with Tom Marino of Boys and Girls Clubs of America and explained what we are trying to accomplish through the formation of our New York Community Advisory Board. He was quite forthcoming about B&GCA's efforts in the Northeast and suggested that we contact the United Way of Tri-State regarding enlisting business executives for our local board. He also helped me to catch up on the many changes that have taken place at B&GCA since I worked there in the early 1980s. Regarding the Junior League, I have asked our New York regional director, Eric Weingartner, to contact them regarding possible volunteers for our New York board. I will also look into our relationship with the Volunteer Consulting Group as a possible source of candidates for our local and national boards.

For your information, I have enclosed a copy of our development plan for FY 1996. I prepared it shortly after my arrival and it still looks to be on track. If anyone at the Fund has any questions or comments, please let me know. As you'll note, the plan includes our upcoming direct mail test which is now scheduled for mailing the last week of March or the first week of April. I will send over sample mailing packages as soon as they are available. We are keeping our fingers crossed that we can succeed in the mail without squarely trespassing on the bounds of good taste!

In closing, I would like to thank you again for the Cummings Memorial Fund's support of Teach For America. The Fund's recent capacity building grant has played a significant role in equipping Teach For America to achieve its goal of becoming a long-standing American institution. I look forward to speaking with you again about continuing this partnership and the submission of a proposal in March for the Fund's consideration.

Sincerely,

Julian Johnson
Director of Development

Ms. Marijane Lundt
Program Officer
Focus on Children
The Prudential Foundation
751 Broad Street
15th Floor
Newark, NJ 07102-3777

Dear Marijane:

I thought that I would use this opportunity to provide you with a brief update on the lead poisoning prevention project. Since my last letter, we have made progress on several fronts:

1. We've written two completely new Spanish songs for the Spanish language version of the audiotape. One song is in a salsa style, the other Tejano. We are confident that these two musical styles will enable us to reach a wide variety of Spanish-speaking people in the U.S.

2. We've recorded the "scratch" version of both the English and Spanish audiotapes for testing. The English version is taken largely from the videotape sound track, with a few "storytelling" devices added. On the Spanish audiotape, Maria tells the story and acts out all the parts. We have researched both versions and have gotten good feedback and good suggestions on how to make the tapes even better.

3. With permission from you, we've hired a project assistant for six months. This is enabling us to stay on top of the myriad of work.

4. We recently made the decision to turn the adult brochure into a comic book with a poster inside. Although this has made this print piece much more complicated to do, we are getting confirmation that this is the way to go. We've retained Ron Zalme, an excellent comic book artist, to help us out, and are currently testing both the English and Spanish versions of the comic.

5. We've formally named the project *Sesame Street* Lead Away! It cleared the legal title search.

6. Although several months away from the official launch of the project, we are capitalizing on opportunities to promote the availability of materials. Staff from our Community Education

Services Department attended the National Association for the Education of Young Children conference where we had a booth for two and a half days. We developed a flyer announcing the project and included a tear off sheet for child care teachers to receive free copies of the package. Interest in the project was significant and we already have a few hundred sign-up slips, most for single copies, but some for multiple copies and a few with offers to help distribute statewide. These efforts will intensify over the next few months.

7. We have also begun discussions with CTW Home Video and have received their initial interest in getting the songs on the radio.

8. Digna Sanchez and Joanne Livesey met with the Executive Director of the National Association of Child Care Resource and Referral Agencies and will be working with them to present the lead poisoning project at several of their regional conferences this spring. In addition, we will arrange for local CCR&Rs to add the materials to their lending libraries and training programs for child care providers.

9. And last but not least, we're moving forward with our plans for the April launch event. As you know, in December staff of our Marketing and Communications Department, Joanne Livesey, and I met with colleagues of yours from Public Affairs at Prudential. The meeting was extremely productive and we were glad to note their enthusiasm in working on this project.

As we near the completion of the project, we remain grateful to you and your colleagues for this opportunity. It's been a lot of hard work, but it's also been a lot of fun. We all feel that the finished materials will be engaging and educational, and will enable us to get the word out about the dangers of lead.

Please let me know if you have any questions. Joanne joins me in sending best wishes.

Yours sincerely,

Ellen S. Buchwalter
[Director]

12

Life after the Grant — or Rejection

The Initial Follow-up to a Grant

You've just received a grant from a foundation or corporation. Congratulations! What should you do? First of all, you should celebrate. Include everyone in your agency who contributed to this wonderful outcome. Thank them for their help and remind them about what this means for your organization.

Next, send a thank-you letter to your funder. This seems so obvious that one would think it hardly worth stating. Yet a number of the grantmakers interviewed for this book responded to the question, "What is the best thing an organization can do after receiving a grant?" with the simple response: send a thank-you letter.

These foundation representatives are expressing a concern that needs to be taken to heart. Appreciate the investment that has just been made in your agency. Recognize that it is not just an institution that is supporting you but the actual people within that institution. Remember that the grants decision makers feel good about the decision to invest in your organization. They may even have had to fight for you in the face of opposition by other staff and board members. Show your thanks and appreciation for this vote of confidence.

Grantmakers want to ensure effective communication after a grant is awarded. They remind us that a grant is a contract to undertake a specific set of activities, and they want and need to know what has transpired.

Remember the watchword of all fundraising: communication. A telephone call to say "Thank you," an update on recent activities, or an announcement of additional funding committed or received are all ways to keep in touch after the grant is made.

Grant Reporting

If a foundation has specific reporting requirements, you will be told what they are. Usually reporting requirements are included in the grant letter; sometimes you are asked to sign and return a copy of the grant letter or of a separate grant contract. These "conditions," which a representative of the nonprofit signs, sometimes require timely reports that are tied to payments.

Here is the Conditions of Grant form used by the Prudential Foundation:

Conditions of Grant

Following are the conditions applying to grants made by The Prudential Foundation (the "Foundation"). You should read these conditions carefully prior to signing this form. Your signature on this form constitutes your acceptance in full of all conditions contained herein. To induce the Foundation to make the grant requested hereby, you (the "grantee") accept and agree to comply with the following conditions in the event that such grant is awarded. As used throughout this form, the term "grant" shall include the income, if any, arising therefrom unless the context otherwise requires.

---

1. PURPOSE AND ADMINISTRATION. The grant shall be used exclusively for the purposes specified in the grantee's proposal, dated _____, the Request for Project Support Form on page 1 hereof, and related documents, all as approved by the Foundation.

   The grantee will directly administer the project or program being supported by the grant and agrees that no grant funds shall be disbursed to any organization or entity, whether or not formed by the grantee, other than as specifically set forth in the grant proposal referred to above.

2. USE OF GRANT FUNDS.

   A. No part of the grant shall be used to carry on propaganda or otherwise attempt to influence legislation within the meaning of Section 4945(d)(1) of the Internal Revenue Code.

   B. No part of the grant shall be used to attempt to influence the outcome of any specific public election or to carry on, directly or indirectly, any voter registration drive within the meaning of Section 4945(d)(2) of the Internal Revenue Code.

   C. No part of the grant shall be used to provide a grant to an individual for travel, study, or similar purpose without complying with the requirements of Section 4945(g) of the Internal Revenue Code as if the grant were made by the Foundation and without prior written approval of the Foundation. Payments of salaries, other compensation, or expense reimbursement to employees of the grantee within the scope of their employment do not constitute "grants" for these purposes and are not subject to these restrictions.

   D. No part of the grant shall be used for a grant to another organization without complying with the requirements of Section 4945(d)(4) and, if applicable, Section 4945(h) of the Internal Revenue Code as if the grant were made by the Foundation and without prior written approval of the Foundation.

   E. No part of the grant shall be used for other than religious, charitable, scientific, literary, or educational purposes or the prevention of cruelty to children or animals within the meaning of Section 170(c)(2)(B) of the Internal Revenue Code.

F. The grantee promptly shall repay any portion of the grant which for any reason is not used exclusively for the purposes of the grant. The grantee shall repay to the Foundation any portion of the grant which is not used exclusively for the purposes described in Section 1 hereof within the time specified in the grantee's proposal or within any approved extension of said time period and, in any case, within fifteen (15) days after such specified time or such extension. If the Foundation terminates the grant pursuant to Section 9 hereof, the grantee shall repay within thirty (30) days after written request by the Foundation all grant funds unexpended as of the effective date of termination and all grant funds expensed for purposes or items allocable to the period of time subsequent to the effective date of termination. In the event that any portion of the grant is used for purposes other than those described in Section 170(c)(2)(B) of the Internal Revenue Code, the grantee shall repay to the Foundation that portion of the grant as well as any additional amount in excess of such portion necessary to effect a correction under Section 4945 of the Internal Revenue Code.

G. If the grantee is directly or indirectly controlled by the Foundation or by one or more "disqualified persons" (within the meaning of Section 4946 of the Internal Revenue Code) with respect to the Foundation, the grantee agrees (i) to expend all of the grant prior to the grantee's first annual accounting period following the taxable year in which the grantee receives a grant payment, thereby permitting the Foundation to count the grant as a qualifying distribution under Section 4942(g)(3) and (h) of the Internal Revenue Code; and (ii) to submit to the Foundation promptly after the close of the grantee's annual accounting period a full and complete written report signed by an appropriate officer, director, or trustee, showing that the qualifying distribution has been made, the name and address of the recipients, the amounts received by each, and that all the distributions are treated as distributions out of corpus.

3. BUDGET. Expenditures of the grant funds must adhere to the specific line items in the grantee's approved grant budget. Transfers among line items (increases and decreases) are permitted under the conditions and to the extent indicated in the Foundation's Budget Preparation Guidelines in effect at the time of any such proposed transfer, and such Budget Preparation Guidelines in their entirety, and as they may be modified by the Foundation from time to time, are incorporated herein by this reference.

4. ACCOUNTING AND AUDIT. The grantee shall indicate the grant separately on its books of account. A systematic accounting record shall be kept by the grantee of the receipt and disbursement of funds and expenditures incurred under the terms of the grant, and the substantiating documents such as bills, invoices, cancelled checks, and receipts, shall be retained in the grantee's files for a period of not less than four (4) years after expiration of the grant period. The grantee agrees promptly to furnish the Foundation with copies of such documents upon the Foundation's request.

The grantee agrees to make its books and records available to the Foundation at reasonable times. The Foundation, at its expense, may audit or have audited the books and records of the grantee insofar as they relate to the disposition of the funds granted by the Foundation, and the grantee shall provide all necessary assistance in connection therewith.

5. REPORTS. Narrative and financial reports shall be furnished by the grantee to the Foundation for each budget period of the grant and upon expiration, repayment (pursuant to Section 2F hereof), or termination of the grant (pursuant to Section 9 hereof). Such reports shall be furnished to the Foundation within a reasonable period of time after the close of the period for which such reports are made. The narrative report shall include a report on the progress made by the grantee towards achieving the grant purposes and any problems or obstacles encountered in the effort to

achieve the grant purposes. The financial report shall show actual expenditures reported as of the date of the report against the approved line item budget. Such reports shall be retained in the grantee's files for a period of not less than four (4) years after expiration of the grant period.

The Foundation may, at its expense, monitor and conduct an evaluation of operations under the grant, which may include visits by representatives of the Foundation to observe the grantee's program procedures and operations and to discuss the program with the grantee's personnel.

6. COPYING, FOUNDATION USE OF DATA, AND PUBLIC USE DATA TAPES. Except as may otherwise be provided in Section 11 hereof, all copyright interests in materials produced as a result of this grant are owned by the grantee. The grantee hereby grants to the Foundation a nonexclusive, irrevocable, perpetual, royalty-free license to reproduce, publish, copy, alter, or otherwise use and to license others to use any and all such materials, including any and all data collected in connection with the grant in any and all forms in which said data are fixed. If the box below is checked, the grantee shall, at no additional cost to the Foundation, cause public use data tape(s) to be constructed (with appropriate adjustments to assure individual privacy) unless the Foundation shall otherwise specify, such public use data tape(s) shall include all data files used to conduct the analysis under the grant.

❏ Public use data tape(s) and full documentation required.

7. PUBLIC REPORTING. The Foundation will report this grant, if made, in its next Annual Report. The Foundation does not usually issue press releases on individual grants; however, should the Foundation elect to do so, it would discuss the press release with the grantee in advance of dissemination. The grantee may issue its own press announcement but shall seek approval of the announcement from the Foundation before distribution. In addition, the grantee will be asked to review and approve a Program Summary briefly describing the grantee's activity which will be used by the Foundation to respond to inquiries and

for other public information purposes. The grantee's approval shall not be unreasonably withheld.

The grantee shall send to the Foundation copies of all papers, manuscripts, and other information materials which it produces that are related to the project supported by the Foundation.

In all public statements concerning the Foundation—press releases, annual reports, or other announcements—the grantee is specifically requested to refer to the Foundation by its full name: The Prudential Foundation.

8. GRANTEE TAX STATUS. The grantee represents that it is currently either (i) a tax-exempt entity described in Section 501(c)(3) of the Internal Revenue Code and either (a) is not a private foundation described in Section 509(a), or (b) is an exempt operating foundation described in Section 4940(d)(2); or (ii) an organization described in Section 170(c)(1) or Section 511(a)(2)(B). The grantee shall immediately give written notice to the Foundation if the grantee ceases to be exempt from federal income taxation as an organization described in Section 501(c)(3) or its status as not a private foundation under Section 509(l), as an exempt operating foundation described in Section 4940(d)(2), or as a Section 170(c)(1) or Section 511(a)(2)(B) organization is materially changed.

9. GRANT TERMINATION. It is expressly agreed that any use by the grantee of the grant proceeds for any purpose other than those specified in Section 170(c)(2)(B) of the Internal Revenue Code will terminate the obligation of the Foundation to make further payments under the grant.

The Foundation, at its sole option, may terminate the grant at any time if (i) the grantee ceases to be exempt from federal income taxation as an organization described in Section 501(c)(3) of the Internal Revenue Code; (ii) the grantee's status as not a private foundation under Section 509(a), its status as an exempt operating foundation under Section 4940(d)(2), or its status as a Section 170(c)(1) or Section 511(a)(2)(B) organization is materially altered; or (iii) in the Foundation's judgment, the grantee becomes unable to carry out the purposes of the grant, ceases to be an appropriate means of accomplishing the purposes of the grant, or fails to comply with any of the conditions hereof.

If the grant is terminated prior to the scheduled completion date, the grantee shall, upon request by the Foundation, provide to the Foundation a full accounting of the receipt and disbursement of funds and expenditures incurred under the grant as of the effective date of termination.

10. LIMITATION; CHANGES. It is expressly understood that the Foundation by making this grant has no obligation to provide other or additional support to the grantee for purposes of this project or any other purposes. Any changes, additions, or deletions to the conditions of the grant must be made in writing only and must be jointly approved by the Foundation and the grantee.

11. SPECIAL CONDITIONS. The grantee accepts and agrees to comply with the following Special Conditions (if no Special Conditions are imposed, so state):

The foregoing conditions are hereby accepted and agreed to as of the date indicated.

Date: _____   Grantee Institution: _____

By _____
(Signature of Authorized Official)

Title: _____

Date: _____   By _____
(Signature of Project Director)

When a foundation provides formal reporting guidelines, in most cases there will be dates when the reports are due. If they have given you specific dates for reporting, develop a tickler system to keep track of them. If you can tell now that you'll have a problem meeting these deadlines (such as your auditors are scheduled for March and the audited financial report is due in February), discuss this with the funder immediately. If the foundation staff has not heard from the grantee within a reasonable time period after the reports are due, they will call or send the grant recipient a note to follow up.

Some funders want reports at quarterly or six-month intervals, but most request an annual report and/or a final report, two to three months after the conclusion of the project. Even for grants of fairly short duration, foundations often express the desire to receive an interim report. Unless otherwise stated, an interim report can be informal.

The W. K. Kellogg Foundation issues very specific reporting instructions. Their most recent *Final Report Guidelines* provide a useful framework to guide agency staff in drafting a report to *any* funder. While these guidelines are designed for the Kellogg Foundation's grantees, as reflected in the references to the commitment letter, outcomes, questions, and implementation questions, they provide a reliable model for reports to other foundations that may not be as specific in their requirements.

The following guidelines are reprinted in their totality with permission from the W. K. Kellogg Foundation:

Final Report Guidelines

The final report from your project to the Kellogg Foundation is an important document. It is a permanent record of what you have achieved and what you have learned in the process. This report helps to shape future grant-making directions for the Foundation.

The final report has two parts. First, it should address the results of the just-completed project year in terms of what was planned, what was accomplished, and what factors helped or hindered the attainment of goals. Second, it represents a thoughtful, critical synthesis of the important lessons learned and outcomes over the life of the project. (See "Project Director's Opinion.")

The format below may help you prepare a final report by providing a checklist for the critical thinking process. You

---

should be especially attentive to addressing, within this format, the important evaluation questions for your project.

Project Summary

This introduction to the full report tells the reader what to expect by "setting the scene." Succinctly restate the project's intended goals, the strategies you have undertaken to achieve them, and the methods by which you are evaluating these efforts. Weave into this brief summary the important questions for evaluation which were stated in your commitment letter. Note if changes have been made in any goals or strategies.

Progress Toward Goals

A. Outcomes
Respond to the specific outcomes questions for your project. In addition, if not already addressed, please consider the following:

1. Summarize your achievements.
2. Does your experience suggest that original expectations for achieving these outcomes were realistic?
3. Have there been any unanticipated outcomes? What are they?

B. Implementation (processes and day-to-day activities)
Respond to the specific implementation questions for your project. In addition, if not already addressed, please consider the following:

1. Describe activities directed at each of the outcomes listed above and lessons you have learned during the life of your project.
2. If some intended activities were not undertaken, please note them and explain why they were not pursued.
3. What problems arose and how were they addressed?
4. Describe any new activities or modifications and why they were added.
5. Share other pertinent observations/accomplishments.

C. Context (characteristics of the setting, needs of targeted groups, and external and internal project conditions that may help or impede project success)

Respond to the specific outcomes for your project. In addition, if not already addressed, please consider the following:

1. Describe factors or circumstances (positive and/or negative) within your environment that affected progress toward achieving your goals.

2. How did relationships with other organizations, institutions, or agencies help or hinder your progress toward addressing needs?

Future Plans

A. Has this project become self sustaining? What activities are being conducted?

B. What structure has been established for the continuation of this project?

C. What indications are there that this project can (or cannot) be adopted elsewhere?

Dissemination (1/2 page)

A. What information from your project has been made available to the field and how?

B. What plans do you have, if any, at this time for disseminating information about your project?

Project Director's Opinion

A. What do you think are the most important outcomes and "lessons learned" from this project?

B. What are the most important lessons that you have learned from this experience?

C. What recommendations would you make to other project directors working in this area or to the Foundation?

Other

Attach to the final report any appendices which will help to clarify information contained in the body of the report. Be selective! Do not include copies of every newspaper article, brochure, or detailed statistics report having to do with the project. If possible, attach a copy of the organizational chart both for the project and for its place within the greater institutional structure. Attach evaluation reports generated during the project if not contained within this report, or submitted with earlier annual progress reports.

The Kellogg Foundation guidelines are particularly applicable if you have received special project support. Don't be concerned if your project does not lend itself to many of these questions. For instance, if you have received $15,000 to hire a tutor for your after-school program, many of these sections, such as "Dissemination," are probably not applicable. Others, like "Future Plans," should be addressed in some fashion in almost any report.

Even if you have received unrestricted, general-purpose support, funders want to know what overall goals you set for your agency for the year. Did you achieve them? What were some particular triumphs? What were some particular problems you faced, and how did you overcome them? Or, are you still dealing with the challenges? (Remember, realism is what counts, along with a sense of confidence that you are appropriately managing the grant.) In contrast to the very specific guidelines from the Kellogg Foundation, the New York Community Trust has these very simple reporting instructions:

A condition of this grant is that you submit to us an interim and a final report. The interim report should be submitted by [six months after date of grant] and a final report by [one year after date of grant]. These reports should contain a fiscal accounting of grant expenditures and a narrative describing the following: (a) the objectives of the project supported by the grant, (b) activities carried out to meet each objective, (c) results accomplished, and (d) any problems encountered and how they were resolved. They should also include a detailed discussion of activities carried out to secure funding to continue this project once our grant expires.

These are presented as general models only. If a foundation supplies its own guidelines, then adhere to those instructions.

Seeking a Renewal

In certain cases, you will want to request that the grant be renewed or that a follow-up project be supported. Some funders refuse to give renewed support because they do not want to encourage dependency or because they see their funding as providing "seed money."

Some funders require a certain period of time to elapse between the grant and the renewal request. For instance, the Hearst Foundations currently require three years between grants, and the Frances L. & Edwin L. Cummings Memorial Fund requests that an agency wait six months after receiving a grant before requesting renewed support.

Even a grant that could be a candidate for renewal may be labeled a one-time gift. Ordinarily the phrase "one-time gift" means that the funder is making no commitment to future funding. It does not necessarily mean that no possibility for future support exists.

If you know that you will want to request renewed support, you should communicate this early on to the foundation in order to determine the best time to submit another request. Be careful not to wait too long before requesting a renewal. By the time the funder receives the request, all the foundation's funds may be committed for the following year.

You should also determine early on the format required by the funder for submitting a renewal request. Some foundations require a full proposal; others want just a letter. This is another illustration of the differences among funders. It reinforces the need to communicate with the grantmaker to determine their particular requirements.

A report on funds expended and results of the first grant is a particularly critical document if you are going to ask for renewed support. However, many funders want your request for renewal to be separate from the report on the grant. In larger foundations, the report and the request for renewal might be handled by different departments; therefore, if you submit your renewal request as part of the report on the first grant, it might not find its way into the proposal system.

Following Up on a Declination

The most important response to a rejection letter is not to take it personally. An old fundraising adage is that "Campaigns fail because people don't ask, not because they get rejected." If your proposal gets rejected, it means you are out there asking. You are doing what you should be doing. Hopefully, you have sent your proposal to a number of other appropriate funders and have not "put all your eggs in one basket." A rule of thumb is that you should approach three funders for every grant you need. Thus, even if one or two prospects turn your proposal down, you still have a shot at the third.

Some funders will talk with you about why the proposal was rejected, particularly if you had a meeting with the program staff at the granting institution prior to or at the time of submission. A phone call following a rejection letter can help you clarify the next step. Your request may have been of great interest to the foundation but was turned down in that funding cycle because the board had already committed all the funds set aside for projects in your subject or geographical area. For example, if your request was for an AIDS program in South Chicago, the foundation may have already committed its grants budget for that geographic area. A call to a foundation staff member might result in encouragement to reapply in a later funding cycle.

All funding representatives emphasize, however, the need to be courteous in the process of calling once you have received a rejection letter. It is never easy to say "no," and a program officer who fought hard for your proposal may feel almost as disappointed as you are that it was turned down. While foundation staff usually want to be helpful, it is important to recognize that it can often be difficult to tell someone why a proposal has been rejected.

Most of the grantmakers interviewed for this guide would agree with Hunter Corbin of the Hyde and Watson Foundation about turn-downs. He said, "There may be a couple of factors, but the usual ones are:

- we run out of money;
- the timing of the application is off;
- the request is vague;
- we are not interested in the subject."

It is important to take your cue from the funder, either from the rejection letter or from the follow-up call to staff. If you are not encouraged to resubmit, then you probably shouldn't.

There are times when a funder will encourage you to resubmit the same request at a particular time in the future. If you have been given this advice, then follow it. In your cover letter, be sure to refer to your conversation with the funding representative, remembering to re-state, but not overstate, the earlier conversation.

Even if a foundation is not interested in funding the particular project you submitted, by keeping the lines of communication open and remaining respectful you will be nurturing the opportunity for future funding. Hildy Simmons of J. P. Morgan & Co., Incorporated reminds us, "Remember, 'no' isn't forever. Be gracious about the turndown. It is okay to call or write for feedback."

Summary Tips

What to do if you receive a grant:
- Send a personalized thank you.
- Keep the funder informed of your progress.
- Follow the funder's reporting requirements.

What to do if your request is turned down:
- Don't take it personally.

- Be sure you understand why.
- Find out if you can resubmit at a later date.

APPENDIX A

What the Funders Have to Say

The 21 grantmakers interviewed for this guide were carefully selected. For continuity's sake we included as many as possible from the prior edition, but several had retired or moved on to new positions. We increased the number of interviewees from both corporate and community foundations and included more funders of the arts and humanities and several that provide capital funding. Our goal was to capture the current proposal processing climate within foundations.

Overview of Responses

The grantmakers interviewed for this guide are very aware of and sensitive to the upheaval going on in the nonprofit world as a result of alterations in funding patterns and especially the loss of federal government support.

They report that they are making subtle changes in the way they award grants to accommodate these special circumstances. For example, general operating support is becoming more common when it becomes clear it will ensure the survival of a well-run nonprofit. And a number of the grantmakers interviewed report increased requests for support for capacity building and endowment from nonprofits who view this type of support as critical to financial stability.

As uncertainty grows, grantmakers are rewarding organizations that are adaptable to change. They are looking for those that exhibit strong infrastructure and board accountability. They are making grants for strategic operations and looking for indications that nonprofit agencies have engaged in careful planning.

A number of the grantmakers interviewed now offer technical assistance to nonprofits to help them conduct self-assessment and to figure out what comes next. They are devoting more resources to assisting nonprofit grantseekers with their applications and to working collaboratively with grant applicants.

As in our prior survey, the funders interviewed indicated that grantmaking is still very much a highly personalized process. Meetings with applicants and especially site visits are increasingly important to grantmakers.

Many expressed frustration at those who do little or no prospect research in advance of submitting a proposal, and at those who try to develop personal relationships with potential donors in lieu of doing their homework and in place of sound proposal preparation.

Evaluation of grant projects is as critical as ever and was referred to fairly often by the grantmakers interviewed, as was the importance of continuing communication once a grant is made. All grantmakers interviewed stressed the importance of establishing a partnership with the grantee and the contract nature of a grant. As one grantmaker was careful to indicate, "a grant is not a gift."

Most of the grantmakers responded favorably to the proposal format outlined in this guide. They provided lots of opinions and personal preferences about formatting of documents, use of brochures, videotapes, and newspaper clippings. Common application forms developed by some regional associations of grantmakers received mixed reviews from this group of grantmakers.

The corporate donors interviewed report that they are finding more ways to involve employees in the grant decision-making process. This is an advantage for grassroots groups that have lots of opportunities for folks to volunteer.

All grantmakers surveyed stated that they seek out nonprofits that are businesslike in their operations and in the manner in which they approach the grantseeking process. Along the same vein, there is recognition on the part of grantmakers that some applicants are becoming more sophisticated in their approach to seeking funding. A few suggested that the earlier edition of this guide and the Foundation Center's related proposal writing seminars have contributed to this trend. They report growing evidence that grantseekers have done their homework and are submitting finely honed proposals.

Technology and Grantmaking

One of the objectives of the survey was to determine how grantmakers are calling on new technologies to assist in the proposal review process. Few of the grantmakers interviewed report that their respective foundations are eagerly embracing computer communication.

All of the grantmakers who participated in the interviews for this book have fax machines, yet most prefer that proposals be sent through the mail. The fax machine is used mainly for follow-up communication or submission of missing information.

Computerization is becoming commonplace in the nonprofit sector. The Internet, and especially the World Wide Web, e-mail, and CD-ROMs are part of the normal workday for many. And most grantmakers report that they are still drowning in paperwork. (One corporate grantmaker said, "The proliferation of paper is overwhelming.") Yet again few of the grantmakers interviewed report regular use of computers to assist in the process. None currently accept proposals electronically on disk or via e-mail. Most seem to feel that accepting proposals via computer is a big step they are not yet ready to take.

While the funding community wants to make the process of securing funding as easy as possible for nonprofit agencies, many believe that computerization does not significantly help their grantees. One expressed the concern that lack of computers puts some grantees at a disadvantage.

Given the large number of grantmakers who nonetheless state that they intend to call upon the computer as an information tool in the future, the next few years seem likely to bring about change in the use of technology by grantmakers.

Here's What the Funders Have To Say:

What trends in grantmaking have you remarked on recently?

We and nonprofits are building new programs based on what we have learned. There is an increase in inquiries, and they are of a higher level. How prudent and persistent nonprofits are! (Alberta Arthurs)

Competition is tougher. Grantees must know and tell us the context they are operating in. We support the most critical programs. Agencies have to make a cogent case and relate it to their operating environment. We are giving very little start-up support and almost no grants to projects that see themselves as models. Evaluation is critical. We want to know what the outcomes will be and how they will be measured. How will agencies recognize their accomplishments? How will they know how they are doing? We are concerned that organizations have stable infrastructures. We still give capacity-building grants. (Joyce Bove)

We are trying to do more to strengthen our side of the process. We make site visits. We now have a "short list" of institutions we want to see. Our new priority is in the arts, focused on small- and medium-sized collections. (John Cook)

We are seeing more appeals and more professional appeals that are sharper, better organized. There are a large number of requests for computer assistance and replacement of hardware and software. We are also seeing the creation of computer labs in educational institutions. (Hunter Corbin)

We are making fewer multiyear grants. But otherwise we are very flexible as to what we fund, such as capital projects and general operating support. (F. Worth Hobbs)

We have better communication with our applicants and donees. We are seeing more nonprofits raising endowment money than in the past. Evaluation of projects will be more important in the future. We will look more closely at a nonprofit's governance function. There has to be a capacity to be accountable for funds given. (Reatha Clark King)

Health and human services organizations are in a "wait and see" position. Their worlds are changing. We are seeing more mergers and collaborations among grantees. We are also seeing lots of strategic planning. (Susan Lajoie)

Government money is scarcer. Hence charities are scrambling. Some are merging. The weaker ones will disappear because they have not done planning. Strategic planning is critical, and often professional staff are not in favor of it. Charities must be run as businesses. More funders seem to be doing site visits, seeing organizations on their own turf. It is a plus if a project is replicable. We might network with other donors about a project. (Andrew Lark)

We are funding more direct service and less policy/advocacy projects. (Marijane Lundt)

Grantseekers are more sophisticated. People are doing excellent research. We will give more general operating support to social service organizations affected by government cuts. There may be some multiyear grants awarded on a case-by-case basis. We are collaborating more with our colleagues, and while we don't wish to push the nonprofits into inappropriate partnerships, we hope they are not reinventing the wheel. (Ilene Mack)

If a nonprofit comes to us and has operating deficits, the application is less competitive. We need to see a recovery plan. Endowments are useful in uncertain times. Many human service agencies tend not to have carefully cultivated donor populations, but, as a category, we are seeing growth in capital campaigns. This suggests a growing capacity to seek voluntary gift support. As a foundation, we encourage voluntary giving. (John Marshall)

We are a proactive, focused donor. We want to see grantees be accountable. (John Mason)

In recent years, 75% of our grants were renewals, and there has been very little room for new initiatives. (Cynthia Merritt)

We are seeing more requests to help an organization hire development staff. (Bruce Newman)

In the corporate setting, grants decision-making is being pushed into the hands of employees more than ever before. (Christine Park)

Application forms are now being used more frequently. We hold orientation sessions at our foundation before every grant cycle. We are amazed at how many people don't attend. Grantseekers don't take advantage of all the opportunities offered by the foundation. (Alicia Philipp)

Matching funds are becoming more important. This is an incentive to get local buy-in and assure future support. We also are awarding more planning grants to give nonprofits time to see if their proposed ideas are feasible. In other words, we want to make sure all the questions have been answered, all the potential benefits and risks have been examined, and there is a clear indication of what will result from an implementation grant. That's why the foundation is willing to make a modest investment up front before committing to an entire project. Finally, we, like other foundations, are becoming much more results oriented. We ask, "What will be different at the end of the grant period?" (Jane Quinn)

General operating support is growing. Other rules are softening. We are providing management assistance grants and cash flow loans. (Julie Rogers)

We will see the downsizing of the sector. We are looking at the impact resulting from the loss of public funding. How do we perform triage? How do we help those, who don't have their heads in the sand, think about the change in the environment? (Hildy Simmons)

There is great uncertainty in the nonprofit world. Grantseekers have to learn to shift focus away from the federal government to their state governments. We are providing: training, technical assistance, and planning grants. (Deborah Wallace)

Nonprofits must learn to focus on positives, not just needs. Also, they must start to think in an integrated, not categorical, manner. (Eugene Wilson)

What is the best initial approach to your foundation/corporation?

The proposal initiates the process at The New York Community Trust. We review the document and then call the grantseeker for a follow-up meeting or if something we need has been left out of the application. We will not penalize a nonprofit for calling as a first step, but because of the complexity of the issues, we really need written materials before a discussion is fruitful. (Joyce Bove)

Let me share a few "nevers" first.
- Never send a cold proposal.
- Never call first.
- Never drop by the office without an appointment.

The grantseeker obviously should do research first. Then, send a letter of inquiry. Tell us how the need corresponds to the published interests of the foundation. (John Cook)

We will take calls as a first step, although the conversation may not shed any special light on the situation. It helps to have a letter of inquiry. Nonprofits that already know the Foundation may prefer to use our application form and forget about the letter of inquiry. (Hunter Corbin)

We must have the proposal, but it plays a limited role with us. We know most of our grantseekers and how they fit into our process. We meet with them to help decide what to submit. (F. Worth Hobbs)

First, get our guidelines and decide if you fit. Then call if you want to chat about the submission. A call is especially helpful if the request is at the upper end of our giving range. Finally, submit the request. (Reatha Clark King)

It is really important for a nonprofit to do research. It is a good idea to obtain our biennial report to be certain we are an appropriate prospect. We prefer targeted applications rather than a shotgun approach. We will be happy to talk about an application over the phone. Then, once a proposal of merit is received, we will meet with the applicant to discuss it. (Andrew Lark)

We want to see a letter of inquiry first. Then we will meet with the nonprofit and help design the proposal. If we receive an unsolicited proposal which is within our areas of interest, we might ask the grantseeker to visit with us to discuss the project in greater detail. (Marijane Lundt)

We are more than happy to have appointments and/or phone conferences leading to the submission of a proposal. (John Marshall)

Either a telephone call or letter of inquiry starts the process. We spend a lot of time working with an organization up front. We only need enough data to be comfortable prior to a meeting. Then a proposal is submitted. We don't respond to unsolicited proposals. (John Mason)

We like to see a brief pre-proposal to start. If we know the grant-seeker, a phone call might work. In the past, we had more staff time. Now, staff might be more responsive to a written approach. (Cynthia Merritt)

Submit a full proposal first. Then you get a postcard indicating receipt of the request. Foundation staff is assigned to each request. They make phone contact and visit with grantseekers. (Bruce Newman)

Do your homework. Are we a logical fit? If you are convinced that is the case, then a call is fine, but you can also just submit the proposal. (Christine Park)

A telephone call first helps us pre-screen for a fit between us and the grantseeker. The nonprofit then fills out our application form and sends it on to us. Staff will chat further with the applicant and probably make a site visit. (Alicia Philipp)

First, the nonprofit should send a query letter. Then a program officer will call the grantseeker to:

- discuss how competitive an application may be;
- explore questions the foundation has;
- determine if a proposal should be sent in.

A proposal, if invited, is the third step. (Julie Rogers)

There just isn't enough time to chat on the phone. We would prefer either a letter or full proposal. (Hildy Simmons)

We ask that grantseekers send a letter of inquiry. If we believe there is a fit, we will get in touch with the grantseeker and request a full proposal. That leads to further conversations and a site visit. (Deborah Wallace)

An agency must commit time to learn about us. The best way is to review our annual report—our signature piece. It announces our focus to the world. Then, the grantseeker should send a letter of introduction. We will ask for a request on our application form, if we believe there is a fit. Staff collects the data and makes a recommendation to the board. (Eugene Wilson)

Generally, we prefer that a grantseeker send a brief letter describing the project. We will review this document, and if we feel there is a fit, then we will invite the grantseeker to visit. Then, a formal request is submitted and reviewed. I want to make a couple of additional points. First, there is no formula here. Sometimes we reach out to the nonprofit and invite an application. Secondly, we want the nonprofit to understand what we do. (Alberta Arthurs)

How do you react to a board member from the grantseeking organization contacting one of your board members directly?

Use every contact you can. (John Cook)

This is fine, if it helps the organization. (Hunter Corbin)

First, this rarely happens. Second, we understand why this occurs in certain circumstances. However, the grant review process is important to our board and the staff. (Susan Lajoie)

At larger foundations, such contacts are often deemed an affront to staff. They are seen as "end runs." It isn't helpful to the grantseeker at our foundation. (Andrew Lark)

I discourage making contact. Our board is a corporate one, and the members are not approachable. (Marijane Lundt)

We work closely with our business units to identify partnerships with nonprofits. So, most grantseekers will not feel the need to contact a board member for help since there is already someone inside the organization lobbying for them. (John Mason)

Our program officers are responsive to comments from a board member. But such interest will not guarantee funding. (Cynthia Merritt)

It is a grantseeker's privilege to contact our board members. (Bruce Newman)

It puts staff in a difficult position when the request is initiated at the board level. (Christine Park)

Staff will never try to prevent this kind of communication. But the board is not tolerant of it. (Alicia Philipp)

If an agency is going to contact a board member, they should communicate that fact to us out of courtesy. The trustees respect the professionalism of the staff and expect us to run the business of the foundation. They set policy and stay out of the business of grantmaking. (Alberta Arthurs)

There are so many grantseekers. If every grantseeker sought the attention of one of our board members, it would be overwhelming for them. The board members do not appreciate this lobbying. It is not necessary to contact board members. The approach should be to staff. (Joyce Bove)

What usually happens when an organization contacts a trustee of your foundation?

The board is courteous toward the staff. They keep their hands off the operation. (Reatha Clark King)

The board typically refers the organization to the staff and informs us. (Susan Lajoie)

Contacting a board member doesn't help. A proposal is reviewed on its merits regardless of who sends it in. (Andrew Lark)

I have never been pressured by a board member. (Marijane Lundt)

Ninety-nine percent of board members will report the contact but generally not advocate on behalf of the nonprofit. (Bruce Newman)

Most board members never tell us. (Alicia Philipp)

Board members will advise prospective grantees of the Fund's review process. In some cases, they may pass information along or ask program staff if they know of the organization that has been in touch. Overall, if program staff follow the guidelines fairly and consistently, the board will back them 100 percent. (Jane Quinn)

Board members will call staff or send a copy of the correspondence, and they will indicate their level of interest. (Julie Rogers)

If a board member is contacted, the communication is sent along to staff without comment. (Joyce Bove; John Mason)

How do you read a proposal? What do you look at first?

I skim the proposal first to understand what the applicant is looking for. Then I read through the entire document. The summary of the proposal is the most important section for me. (Hunter Corbin)

I read the proposal thoroughly the first time, eliminating the need for multiple reads. (Reatha Clark King)

We usually review the executive summary and the budget first. (Susan Lajoie)

I carefully read the cover letter, where I expect to find a concise statement about the project. Then I look at the budget. Only when I am satisfied that the project is within our scope do I then turn to the nuts and bolts. Given the volume of paper we receive, this is an effective short cut. (Andrew Lark)

I skim first. Then go back and read in detail. The executive summary is a key document for me. (Marijane Lundt)

The executive summary is useful to understand the shape of what we are being asked to fund. Then I move on to the need and the project description. This should tell me how the project fits into the foundation's priorities and who is involved. The budget is not a prime consideration during initial screening. (Cynthia Merritt)

In our office, the document is read from beginning to end. The executive summary is key. It should tell us what is being requested and why. (Bruce Newman)

The cover letter should pique my interest. Then I look at the executive summary. It can make or break the request for me. I will spend more time on other sections of the document, if the executive summary convinces me it fits into our priorities. (Christine Park)

Staff reads the entire application. They expect to find a sense of the nonprofit's mission. (Alicia Philipp)

The key document is the executive summary. If goals and strategies aren't crisp and clear, the rest of the proposal won't be either. (Jane Quinn)

I read a document from beginning to end. The cover letter is important to help me get a sense of the project. (Julie Rogers)

I scan the document but pay special attention to the financial data. From that information, I will pick up red flags, ascertain that the organization is not dependent on just one funder, and learn what our money will do. (Hildy Simmons)

I look for and study the grant's objectives. (Deborah Wallace)

At our foundation, proposals are first scanned to determine if they should be rejected or considered further. If we are looking further at the request, the methods section is important. It should tell us how the project is integrated with the work of other nonprofits. We are looking for grantees to break out of categorical thinking. (Eugene Wilson)

I skim the entire document. (Alberta Arthurs)

I look at the problem statement and the plan for addressing it before I read anything else. (Joyce Bove)

We recommend that a proposal be composed of: a cover letter; a proposal narrative with executive summary, need statement, project description including evaluation, budget, fact sheet for the applicant, conclusion; an appendix with board list, IRS designation letter, and financial documents. Is this what you look for?

The numbers said to be "served" by a project should be *realistically* presented. We examine this critical aspect very, very carefully. (Andrew Lark)

The case must be made in the materials. (John Marshall)

These are excellent guidelines. I wish all our applications looked like this. (Cynthia Merritt)

It should include who else funded the organization and the amount, along with a board list including affiliations. We prefer multiyear documents and a project budget projected into the future. (Christine Park)

It is really important to be clear about the need statement. It is the compelling nature of the need that gets attention. (Julie Rogers)

In addition to the above, it is also helpful if the proposal indicates who else is doing similar work in the community. (Deborah Wallace)

There is no formula. It depends on the project, the agency, and the funder. Often the proposal writer starts with information about the applying organization. That doesn't help us in figuring out how much support the agency needs and why. (Alberta Arthurs)

Often agencies don't address our guidelines. Therefore items are missing from the application. Or they ask for general operating support, which we ordinarily don't give. (Joyce Bove)

The proposal narrative should contain clarity of concept and demonstrate the organization's capacity to fulfill its objectives. The budget should be detailed and professional. (John Cook)

We look for a nuts-and-bolts description: how it fits us as donor and the agency's mission. The proposal should show the capability of an agency to do the job. Included should be a copy of the organization's Form 990-PF that it files with the IRS. (Reatha Clark King)

What is the best way to present a project budget?

Our grants may support a one-day conference or a multiyear institutional project, so the budgets will vary in presentation. The budget should include the right amount of detail, and it should let us see the total cost of the project and how the foundation's money will be used. (Cynthia Merritt)

Nonprofits often need help constructing a budget. Through the Nonprofit Resource Center we provide technical assistance on budgeting. (Alicia Philipp)

We want to see revenue, not just expense. We require a lot of specificity. Other potential donors with requested dollar amounts should be included. (Julie Rogers)

Grantseekers should put their emphasis here, but be careful not to pad the budget. Too often, we don't receive enough data. (John Cook)

The budget should provide a good picture of the real cost of the program, while avoiding extreme minutiae. It should indicate what percentage of the overall agency budget a specific project represents. Grantseekers should ask for overhead support, but it must be reasonable. (Andrew Lark)

What materials should be included in the appendix?

Included in the appendix should be a copy of the organization's audit, a donor list, a budget, and a copy of their 501(c)(3) certification. (F. Worth Hobbs)

A list of other funders you are asking to support this project. Also provide a list of prior donors (if any) to the same project, on a year-by-year basis. (Andrew Lark)

We look for biographies and educational background of principal staff, and we try to determine what is going on at the organization. (Marijane Lundt)

Include any publications that clarify the organization's governance or sources of support, such as annual reports or audited financial statements. Let us know how other project fundraising is going, including fundraising strategy—that is, whom else you are asking. Remember: funders do talk to each other. (Cynthia Merritt)

Board affiliations and letters of support. (Julie Rogers)

I like what you suggest for the appendix. (John Cook)

There should be a board list with affiliation and titles and a list of other funders (somebody who knows the agency). (Hunter Corbin)

The appendix contains backup documents which you need for your review of the proposal. Do you also like to see brochures, videotapes, and newspaper clippings?

Don't bother sending brochures or videos. *One* newsclipping would be okay. It may help me when I do a write-up about the agency for the board. (Ilene Mack)

Supplemental information can always be sent later. Don't give us ten pounds of material, so there isn't anything additional we could possibly want. (John Mason)

It is okay to send any of this, although videotapes are less useful except in the case of media projects. Brochures or publications may be especially relevant. (Cynthia Merritt)

Don't bother sending videotapes. We don't look at them. We might review a brochure or newsclipping when relevant to the proposal. Otherwise, we don't pay attention to them. (Bruce Newman)

In your cover letter, tell me you have a videotape and offer to send it rather than including it. (Christine Park)

Do include an annual report. It can provide useful information; the same goes for newsclippings. Don't send videos. (Alicia Philipp)

An annual report may provide a sense of financial health, and a brochure might have good photos to convey a sense of the people being served. (Jane Quinn)

I rarely look at videos. You could include a few photos. I do like to see brochures and newsclippings. (Julie Rogers)

Newsclippings and brochures should be included *only* if there is something compelling and extraordinary that they convey. (Hildy Simmons)

Keep excess materials to a minimum. They are not looked at. An annual report can help. I will review a video if it is appropriate to an arts application. Please don't send newsclippings, especially if they don't relate to the subject of the proposal. (Alberta Arthurs)

You can send brochures and newsclippings but only if directly related to the proposal. I don't review videos. Further, I see a videotape and think, "This agency has a lot of money to waste." (Joyce Bove)

Many of our donees are already well known to us. We have files on them. Grantseekers always send too much material. Sometimes a brochure or annual report or newsclipping will be helpful. I seldom look at videos. (John Cook)

Brochures and newsclippings might be reviewed. Don't send too many. Be certain they are relevant to the application. Mark the appropriate sections. I rarely look at videos and do not return them unless an envelope is provided. (Hunter Corbin)

We are flexible. We leave what to include to the judgment of the applicant. We are looking for their passion. If these extra materials will help, great. (Reatha Clark King)

We don't want to see slick brochures or a video. Our office does not have a VCR. Newsclippings might be helpful if they relate to the proposal. Be sure to highlight the pertinent areas. It is good cultivation to periodically send newsclippings and other information to donors and prospects. (Andrew Lark)

Brochures are okay, but not newsclippings or videos. I don't have the time to look at videos. (Marijane Lundt)

How should proposals be assembled?

The document should be a standard size. It should be held together with clips, or stapled. Please do not bind it. (Bruce Newman)

Fancy binding, shiny folders, bells and whistles aren't necessary. "Undress" the proposal. (Christine Park)

Do not bind it. Send what is asked for by the potential donor. Be selective about including any additional information. (Jane Quinn)

We accept whatever the nonprofit does in putting the proposal package together. However, a flashy presentation doesn't impress us. (Alberta Arthurs)

Expensive binding of the document is a turnoff. (Joyce Bove)

This is not much of an issue for us. We do prefer use of staples, clips, and loose-leaf notebooks. Don't bind the document. This makes it hard for us to handle. (John Cook)

Staple everything, even the audit. (Hunter Corbin)

Binding the document is attractive only to the sender. Use staples to hold it together. (Reatha Clark King)

Don't tightly bind the document as it must be easy to take apart. Use elastic bands, clips, or staples. Be sure the pages are clearly numbered. Finally, send the number of copies requested—not more or less. Extra copies are thrown out. (Susan Lajoie)

What should the cover letter include?

The cover letter is a letter of transmittal. It should include the following information: two to three sentences about the project; an indication of the total cost and the amount requested of us; and the contact person if different from the signer. (Susan Lajoie)

The cover letter is a letter of transmittal. It should be an overview of the proposal. (Marijane Lundt)

The cover letter builds on personal contact. It should be brief and comprehensive. (John Mason)

It should ask me for a specific sum, remind me of a past relationship, if one exists, and give me detail on the project. But be brief. (Cynthia Merritt)

This is a summary of what you plan to do and should include the specific amount you are seeking from us. (Jane Quinn)

It is a summary of your project. (Deborah Wallace)

It should be a summary of the data. Otherwise, we will not review it. Tell us what other donors are involved. Be specific about a request to us. (Eugene Wilson)

It should be a transmittal document and include a specific dollar request. (John Cook)

Grantseekers should put key information here. The letter should tell me who you are, how your agency fits our guidelines, and how much you are seeking. (Hunter Corbin)

This is the formal request. It is important and should be developed carefully. It should include a specific dollar request. (F. Worth Hobbs)

The cover letter is a summary of what we will find in the request. Be sure to ask for a specific dollar amount. (Reatha Clark King)

How long should the cover letter be?

One and one-half pages would be perfect. (Julie Rogers)

It doesn't matter. (F. Worth Hobbs)

One page would be great. (Susan Lajoie)

Anything up to one and one-half pages is fine. (Andrew Lark)

I don't pay attention to the length. (Cynthia Merritt)

Who should sign the cover letter?

We have no rule about who signs the cover letter. However, if we are seriously considering awarding a grant, we send the agency a "Conditions of a Grant" document, which must be reviewed and accepted by the board chair and the CEO jointly. (Marijane Lundt)

I don't have hard and fast rules here. If the CEO signs an application, it indicates involvement from the top of the organization. But be certain to tell me whom to call for specific information about the project. (Ilene Mack)

I expect the CEO to write the letter and to assure the funds will be used as intended. It is not fair to impose this task on the board chair, and the director of development doesn't have the necessary authority. (Bruce Newman)

Who is in charge? That person should sign the letter. In big institutions, the development staff usually sign, but tell me whom to contact about the project. (Hildy Simmons)

We want to know that there is institutional support for a project, so the most relevant professional involved with the project would be fine. (Alberta Arthurs)

The letter should be signed by the CEO. This person should know about and approve the application. (Joyce Bove)

We need to know that the board is aware of the project. We request that the board chair or an appropriate officer on behalf of the applicant's governing board sign the application. (Hunter Corbin)

It is the joint responsibility of the board and the executive director to implement a project when we fund it. Hence, I expect dual signatures of the CEO and board chair. This shows that responsible parties are in support of the request. (Susan Lajoie)

We want total agency buy-in around a project, but we are flexible as to who signs the letter. It is dangerous to just append a cover letter to a proposal written by staff or by a consultant if the proposal doesn't truly reflect the agency and what it is capable of accomplishing. (Andrew Lark)

What is the preferred length of a proposal?

I believe it takes various organizations different lengths to articulate what they want and who they are. (Christine Park)

The shorter the better, but no more than 10 pages. I like reasonably big typeface and proposals that are double spaced. (Julie Rogers)

Ten pages, but keep it under 15. We prefer less rather than more. (John Cook)

Short enough to show consideration for our time. (Reatha Clark King)

I prefer seven to eight pages. If an organization is submitting two requests to us, they should not repeat the data about their agency in the second request. (Andrew Lark)

Under 10 pages. (Marijane Lundt)

A one- or two-page summary with no more than five pages in the full proposal. (Ilene Mack)

How important is the proposal's layout?

I have high expectations of all of our applicants. Reason, logic, and substance should prevail in the document. Extract data in such a way that it is easy to get through. It must be readable. (Hildy Simmons)

Use whatever formatting techniques will break-up the density of the page. Don't single space! (Deborah Wallace)

The more professional the proposal looks, the better. Use your in-house computer capability, rather than using an outside printer to produce your materials. (Eugene Wilson)

The layout can help the reader. Use underlines, bullets, and indentations to indicate the next subject. (Alberta Arthurs)

The layout makes it easier to read. It enables you to impress the reader with the content of your work. (Joyce Bove)

A lot should be invested in the way a proposal is presented and how it looks. Use bullets. Don't single space. Please remember, though, that the clarity of the argument you are presenting is critical. Lastly, keep in mind that we like to underline and make notes. Give us the space to do that. (John Cook)

If you write too much, it can be unclear. (Hunter Corbin)

Layout is very important. Organize the document so it is not boring or confusing to read. (Reatha Clark King)

Layout is important in facilitating readability. However, we look beyond the written word. We can gain understanding of people and capacity from interviews and site visits. (Susan Lajoie)

If the document is well thought out and well organized, it can help the reader. Use bullets, too. We are not looking for a slick, glossy document. We will overlook a less polished look if the "meat" of the idea is present. (Andrew Lark)

Using bullets to make a point makes the nonprofit seem businesslike. (Marijane Lundt)

The layout should make reading easy, but grantseekers should avoid fancy doodads. (Ilene Mack)

The layout makes it easy for us to read. This includes good organization, like a table of contents. Indent. Use bullets. A busy reader's eye jumps to these points. Also consider blocking and single-spacing some data. (Cynthia Merritt)

Do what will be helpful for the reader. Use bullets and other formatting techniques. I do want to point out that we do not care about the quality of the writing. If the information is there, that's all we are concerned about. (Bruce Newman)

Leave space for jottings by the reader. (Christine Park)

Double-spacing helps. (Julie Rogers)

What is the primary reason a proposal succeeds in being funded?

First, we funded the agency before. We like their work and are comfortable with them. Second, it's just the luck of the draw. Third, the project was different, neat, or quirky. Fourth, is timing—the application came in at the right time and the agency was responsive with additional information. (Hunter Corbin)

Because it is a good program conducted by good people at the right price per client served. (Andrew Lark)

It isn't just what is in the proposal, but also that the request fits the funder. (Cynthia Merritt)

Because we find the organization's work compelling. (Julie Rogers)

What is the major reason a proposal fails?

One reason we may reject a project is our own lack of resources. A second is a lack of clarity in the proposal about how the project will unfold or how the pieces will come together. (Julie Rogers)

I can think of three reasons. The project is outside of our guidelines, the quality of the project is poor, and/or the cost per client served is unacceptably high. (Andrew Lark)

A big problem can be inadequate research on the part of the applicant. That is to say, they applied to the wrong funder. (Cynthia Merritt)

What is the best thing an organization can do after receiving a grant?

Please say thank you for the grant. (Alicia Philipp)

The best thing you can do is to meet, or even exceed, the goals we agreed to. (Jane Quinn)

Acknowledge the gift quickly. Checks can get sent to the wrong place; we want to know you received the grant. Meet the objectives of the project. (Deborah Wallace)

Work to meet the objectives of the project and to ensure future funding. (Joyce Bove)

Let us see planned publicity about our award in advance. (John Cook)

We send a form that requests information; respond on quickly as possible. Take care of this first. Then send a personalized expression of thanks. (Hunter Corbin)

First, be a good "partner." Help us stay up-to-date on the program. Second, apply the grant to what was promised and do that well. Lastly, let us know about any problems. (Reatha Clark King)

A grant is a contract between the foundation and the nonprofit. So, keep us posted with good and bad news. We will help if a problem arises. Be sure to follow the reporting schedule. (Susan Lajoie)

A quick thank you note would be nice, incorporating a promise of semiannual updates. (Andrew Lark)

We keep grantees aware of what is going on with the review of their request. When the board has made a decision, I call and tell them what happened. If the news is good, first I want them to be happy and then eager to get on with the project. (Marijane Lundt)

I hope for an immediate thank you and then updates about what is happening. (Ilene Mack)

Keep us aware of progress with the project. Be available to answer questions. (Cynthia Merritt)

First, I want a grantee to meet the obligations of the grant. Then, keep the program officer informed. (Bruce Newman)

An important component of a partnership is to regularly communicate about the project. Give us, as the donor, appropriate visibility. (Christine Park)

What is the worst thing an organization can do after receiving a grant?

If you have an effective working partnership with a donor, there's little that can or will go wrong. (Deborah Wallace)

Not keeping us informed, on their mailing list, or invited to events. (Alberta Arthurs)

To not be honest. That would include surprising us or letting us hear from someone else about bad news. Equally problematic would be to unilaterally change the terms of the grant agreement. We know there can be a problem, that things don't always go as planned. But tell us. We will help figure out what to do and troubleshoot. (Joyce Bove)

It is a real negative if the agency fails to respond to our grant letter. (Hunter Corbin)

I see three possible problem areas: first, failure to deliver agreed-upon objectives of the grant; second, not reporting to us, especially if there are problems; third, being overly nervous. We need each other. This is a partnership. Don't be timid about asking for help. (Reatha Clark King)

The worst thing is a breach of trust. That includes: not using the grant as it is supposed to be used; not telling us bad news; letting us read about it in the newspaper. (Ilene Mack)

Two things bother us. An agency gets a grant and then ignores the project. Even worse is challenging us, the funder, about having given too little money. That seems ungrateful. (John Mason)

Not communicating is a problem. Equally bad is not filing the appropriate reports or doing so late. (Bruce Newman)

A failure to say thank you is poor form, but rote computer letters are just as bad. (Julie Rogers)

The biggest issue is a failure to communicate. For example, not telling us about a change in leadership, financial or other problems. We don't want special treatment—just keep us apprised of what is going on. (Hildy Simmons)

What should nonprofits know about reporting on a grant?

We have a timetable for reporting. But the actual documents come in every size and shape. We even have to chase after some agencies to get their reports. (Alberta Arthurs)

Reporting is an important component of our evaluation process. Lessons learned inform future grantmaking. The information on each grant is shared with our board. We report to our board two years after a grant is completed. (Joyce Bove)

We look for an annual report on progress and a summary report. (John Cook)

We need to know right away if there is a delay in implementing a grant. Otherwise, we require six-month and one-year reports. We want grantees to be honest and realistic. Are you meeting expectations or not? We might be able to help put a project back on track. (Andrew Lark)

For many years we did not ask for reports. Today, for endowment and capital awards, payment of the gift is closely tied to reporting. Other single-year grantees, who want to come back in three years to request additional support, would be wise to keep us informed. (Ilene Mack)

A report is expected on the anniversary of the grant. If the project is derailed, we want to know. (John Mason)

We set up a schedule of reports with the grantee. We especially want to know what has been accomplished and the plan to sustain the project. (Cynthia Merritt)

Do you make repeat grants?

We have no criteria as to how often an organization may apply. We tell nonprofit staff that they should request support every year. However, if no award is made in three or four years, we are sending a message. (Hunter Corbin)

We will make another gift based on the qualitative and financial success of the project to date. (Susan Lajoie)

Grantees are requested to wait six months. (Andrew Lark)

We do make repeat grants, but the nonprofit needs to be realistic about what the grantmaker can fund, how long a foundation will support a project, and how much money it can provide. Multiple sources of support and a plan to sustain the project are indicative of good planning and strengthen a case for renewal. (Cynthia Merritt)

Many of our awards are long term, such as three and even six years. We only consider additional grants—what we call second-level funding—if a grantee's performance has been excellent and the grantee proposes work that will build on and strengthen what it accomplished with our first grant. (Jane Quinn)

Can the report and request for additional support be in the same document?

The new proposal can be a vehicle to bring us up to date. We will still need a report. (Susan Lajoie)

The report and the request should be separate documents. They are handled differently at the foundation. (Cynthia Merritt)

They can be one document, although this makes our paperwork complicated. (Bruce Newman)

We predicate the renewal on the report. (Hildy Simmons)

Yes, provided the request deals with the next phase of the work being reported on. (Alberta Arthurs)

What is the best thing an organization can do after being turned down?

If we grantmakers have done our job in explaining our foundation's guidelines and funding interests, a decline should not come as a surprise. A thank you letter is thoughtful, but not necessary. Chat with the program officer about what to do next. (Deborah Wallace)

Send a thank you letter. This might make us feel better. Then come back. We like to see persistence based on a passion for the work. Of course, applicants should pick up clues when their agency isn't appropriate for our foundation. (Alberta Arthurs)

Review our guidelines and try again. Call and discuss the turndown with us. (Joyce Bove)

Call and talk with us about the rejection. We will be honest and make suggestions about next steps. (Hunter Corbin)

Meet with the program officer to discuss the reasons for the declination. (Susan Lajoie)

Find out from us what we viewed as the strengths of your application and why you were not funded. (Marijane Lundt)

Write to me. I might then call to discuss next steps. (Ilene Mack)

Our applicants are aware of the likelihood of support every step of the way. They know grants are made to a small percentage. If there was a rejection, there was probably a good reason for it. Ask for coaching about how to make the application better. (John Mason)

Ask for honest feedback. Listen to it. (Jane Quinn)

Send a letter, thanking us for our consideration and asking for feedback on whether reshaping the proposal is useful. (Julie Rogers)

What is the worst thing an organization can do after being turned down?

It would be terrible if it never applies again. (Joyce Bove)

Argue with us. (John Cook; Marijane Lundt; Christine Park)

Be argumentative on the phone. (Hunter Corbin)

Grantseekers should not assume that rejection means that there is no possibility in the future of a relationship with us, especially if the organization's mission fits our guidelines. (Reatha Clark King)

They should not submit the exact same proposal again. Nor should they avoid applying again with a revised or different proposal. (Susan Lajoie)

Grantseekers should not take the rejection personally and get angry. (Ilene Mack)

They should not take the rejection and go away, and fail to follow-up with us about it. (John Mason)

Grantseekers should not "bad mouth" us. (Alicia Philipp)

Grantseekers should not take it personally or try to do an "end run" around staff by appealing directly to board members. (Jane Quinn)

Grantseekers should not be argumentative or too persistent. When you get a response from us, know when to back off. (Hildy Simmons)

Do resubmitted proposals sometimes get funded?

This may happen, but we don't have the staff time to help the non-profit reshape the request. (Eugene Wilson)

Yes, but usually not from the exact same document. (John Cook)

Occasionally the proposal may be revised and come back to us in time for the same board meeting. (Hunter Corbin)

This can happen, especially if the original request had a good idea but the proposal was not strong. (Marijane Lundt)

Grantseekers have to wait one year between applications. I will suggest they call first. There is a fine line between persistence and pestering. (Ilene Mack)

Often when we say no to a request, it has nothing to do with the proposal, but rather with the organization. If the problem has been fixed, a grant in the future may be forthcoming. (Alicia Philipp)

This has happened plenty of times, usually with refinement and strengthening of the original idea. Persistence, timing, and reconceptualizing are all important. (Jane Quinn)

Grantseekers have to wait a year and reshape the proposal. (Julie Rogers)

Do you permit a request to be submitted via fax?

Yes, a rough draft of the proposal can be faxed. (John Cook)

Proposals can be faxed, but a good copy of the 501(c)(3) letter must follow by mail. (Reatha Clark King)

We appreciate receiving updated information by fax prior to a visit or our board meeting, but not full proposals. (Andrew Lark)

We accept faxed proposals and other data. (Christine Park)

Faxed proposals do not look very good. Anyway, we need several copies of the proposal. (Jane Quinn)

We prefer not to receive requests this way, but have not ruled it out. (Hildy Simmons)

Yes, proposals can be faxed, but we prefer a hard copy. (Alberta Arthurs)

Do you communicate with grantseekers via computer?

We are not currently involved with the Web or Internet, nor do we have plans to be. We do not expect to accept proposals via computer. (Hunter Corbin)

We do not have a home page, but plan to do so. We will weigh the issue of accepting proposals via computer in the future. (F. Worth Hobbs)

Staff is looking into all of this. I doubt we will accept proposals via computer in the immediate future. (Susan Lajoie)

We are part of Prudential's home page and are looking into the rest of it. I am not opposed to proposals via computer, but it is a big step. (Marijane Lundt)

We are investigating all of this. We plan to be on the Internet and may accept proposals via computer. (Ilene Mack)

We are looking into it. If we have the technological capacity, we may accept proposals via computer, but we want to be receptive to the agency that lacks it, too. The difference between instantaneous communication and overnight mail tends to be not much in a five-month application process. (John Marshall)

We are quite far along in this arena. We have a home page on the Web and information available on the Internet, but we have no current plans to receive proposals via computer. (Cynthia Merritt)

We are thinking about what we should do. If it is convenient for grantseekers, we will allow computer submissions. (Christine Park)

We are thinking and talking about what to do. This is not a high priority for us. (Alicia Philipp)

We are investigating what to do. While we now have a Web page, we probably won't allow applicants to submit via computer. (Jane Quinn)

We expect to be on the Web and to have internal and limited external e-mail. I don't expect we will allow proposals via computer. (Hildy Simmons)

We are on the World Wide Web and have an e-mail address. Proposals must be mailed to us, however. We still want the paper. (Alberta Arthurs)

We are in the midst of a major computer reorganization and are thinking about these issues. However, we don't plan to accept proposals electronically. (Joyce Bove)

The foundation is on the Internet and uses e-mail. We will accept drafts of a proposal via computer, but need the hard copy for the final document. (John Cook)

Do you accept/require proposals following a common application form?

No, it makes more work for us to assemble the data that we need, and it encourages nonprofits to take a shotgun approach, rather than carefully researching individual foundation prospects. (Andrew Lark)

No. Give us what we ask for, not the form. (Marijane Lundt)

Yes, we prefer it. (Julie Rogers)

Yes, we accept these proposals, but this has caused agencies to become lax about their research. For example, we do not give general operating support, yet we get applications on the common form for it. (Joyce Bove)

We modified the format created by the local regional association of grantmakers. (Hunter Corbin)

What are your pet peeves?

Letters beginning with "Dear Administrator," signaling that the organization is fishing, not taking the process seriously. Addressing me as "Mr. King." A mismatch between letter and proposal, i.e., when I receive a cover letter addressed to me and a proposal addressed to another foundation. (Reatha Clark King)

Sloppiness concerning the finances. Extraneous material not central to the request. It takes so long to find the "meat." (Susan Lajoie)

Hype, especially when it involves exaggerated numbers "served." (Andrew Lark)

Trying to get close to the donor personally. I don't need to be personally massaged. You shouldn't have to manipulate foundation/corporate staff. (Ilene Mack)

Poor research. I am disappointed by the number of cold calls we get asking us to explain our program. Or, when the project gets done but the agency missed using the opportunity to: strengthen the board; build skills in fundraising; expand the donor base. (John Marshall)

When the applicant clearly has sent out a blanket proposal that does not fit our program, is rejected, and then calls to find out why. (Cynthia Merritt)

You can't find the dollar request in the proposal or worse, the grant-seeker indicates we should send them "whatever you can afford"! The nonprofit just takes its government agency request, changes the name, and submits it to us. (Bruce Newman)

The overly persistent person who calls every week, once per week, to learn if we made a decision. (Christine Park)

Not living up to the contractual relationship. A grant is not a gift. (Alicia Philipp)

Failure to do your homework. (Jane Quinn)

Tiny print. Bound proposals. (Julie Rogers)

These are hard times for all of us. We need a good proposal, otherwise there is nothing we can do. (Hildy Simmons)

Uninformed presumption. Grantseekers should do their homework. We cannot be all things to all people. (Eugene Wilson)

An agency that complains it can't get money out of the Trust, yet has never applied. Grantseekers should not act based on others' experiences. Each nonprofit is unique. (Joyce Bove)

The nonprofit representative who relies on personality to sway the donor. Usually this person is not adequately prepared and behaves in a manner that is too informal and unbusinesslike or uses the appointment to butter us up. (John Cook)

Don't wait until the cutoff date to send in an application. Don't indicate that someone suggested you write if that person did not do so. We get a request signed by the chair but there is no indication of whom to contact at the agency. Failing to endorse a grant check for deposit. Being nasty or pushy. Don't promise you will call in your letter and then not call. (Hunter Corbin)

Do you have any general comments on the proposal process that you'd like to share with grantseekers?

We are process driven. Our field representatives make recommendations to us. We meet, talk, and visit based on these suggestions. We deal with organizations where we have linkages. Therefore, the structure, format, and content of a proposal is secondary. We are proactive. We look at an institution and try to figure out how they fit into our process. (F. Worth Hobbs)

When large organizations apply, they sometimes fail to include information on their parent organization and the division raising the funds. Realize that "campaigns" might be a red herring to some donors. Show why they are important. No matter how difficult, we all need to try to keep the process from becoming overly bureaucratic. Good relationships are built on trust. We send to our board, as part of the review process, a data sheet of up to two pages with staff recommendations. It also includes: history/mission, services, objectives, grant request, governance, and finance information. (Reatha Clark King)

I can't overemphasize the importance of laying out the case in clear, straightforward fashion. There should be no mystery. State who, what, when, where, why with clarity. Simplicity and conciseness are called for rather than using language to sound impressive. There is a growing emphasis on accountability and impact. Be clear about objectives in any discussion that takes place. (Susan Lajoie)

We are wrestling with the issue of general operating versus special project support. We are cutting some slack and working carefully with organizations, especially in periods of fiscal crisis. (Andrew Lark)

Funders need help too. There is risk involved in our work, and our performance is judged by our board. Therefore, we have to be sensitive to "political" issues. If there is potential for conflict, grantseekers should communicate that up front. Grantmakers don't like surprises. (Marijane Lundt)

We participate in fundraising conferences and offer workshops on how to apply to the foundation. We have found this brings in better applications. It also discourages applications when the situation doesn't fit. Grantseeker and donor can have a productive phone call when both sides are knowledgeable. For us grantseeking means: a carefully conceived strategy; a project with organizational enhancement; discipline in implementing the process. (John Marshall)

Do your homework. It is key. Be aggressive—up to the point of annoying the funder. (Christine Park)

There should be less focus on problems and more on opportunities. What assets does an agency have? (Alicia Philipp)

There has been a sea change in government support of nonprofits. Nonprofits are trying to figure out what to do. We're struggling as well. (Julie Rogers)

We look for: good leadership; how the organization fits into the universe; stewardship on the part of the executive director and board. (Hildy Simmons)

The grantseeker's job is difficult. The key is that funders and grantseekers are partners. We both need each other to be successful. I view a grant as a contract. There are mutual expectations and responsibilities. (Deborah Wallace)

We deal with organizations large and small but not solely with the development offices. We want to see the people who function to make the agency strong. (Alberta Arthurs)

Pay enough attention to deadlines. Grantseekers need to tell us what will happen if our board doesn't provide support. (John Cook)

Pictures may be helpful; occasionally they help us to visualize a project. Highlight what aspects of the proposal you want us to focus on. A good board plus a good executive director equal good programs. (Hunter Corbin)

Appendix B

Sample Proposal

January 1, 1997

Andrea L. Correll
Executive Director
Good Works Foundation
Philanthropic Avenue
New York, NY 10000

Dear Ms. Correll:

I am pleased to contact you to introduce the Good Works Foundation to Mind-Builders' work with young women and their families from the Northeast Bronx and to request support for our **Family Services Center.**

Mind-Builders Family Services Center provides intensive counseling and support services, accessible 24 hours a day, to women at risk of having their children removed from the home and placed in foster care. Family Services Center counselors and assistants work with young mothers to help them learn to overcome problems such as spousal abuse and alcohol and/or drug addiction that threaten to break up their families. The caseloads are kept small (40 girls and women a year) enabling the Family Services Center to provide an effective and cost efficient alternative to foster care services.

Our project budget for this year is $358,281. To date, we have secured a $300,000 lead grant from the Child Welfare Administration and have received one generous commitment of $25,000 for this project from the Alternative Trust. To meet our budget, we must raise $33,281 from the private sector. Mind-Builders has approached a number of foundations to provide this support. A list of requests pending review with amounts requested is included in the appendix to our proposal.

We request a grant of $10,000 from the Good Works Foundation to enable the Family Services Center to help girls and young women rebuild their families and their lives. Enclosed please find a proposal describing our program in detail. Please feel free to call me if you have any questions or if you would like to arrange to visit the Family Services Center.

Sincerely,

Camille Giraud Akeju
Executive Director

MIND-BUILDERS FAMILY SERVICES CENTER

Empowering Young Mothers to Maintain Strong Families

A Request for Funding Submitted to the
Good Works Foundation

by

Camille Giraud Akeju
Executive Director

Mind-Builders Family Services Center
3415 Olinville Avenue
Bronx, New York 10467-5612
(718) 652-6256

TABLE OF CONTENTS

EXECUTIVE SUMMARY

At Mind-Builders, we believe that family is our community's most precious resource. In 1992, in response to the needs of the growing numbers of young girls and women in our community faced with the breakup of their families and removal of their youngsters to foster care, Mind-Builders initiated the Family Services Center.

The Family Services Center provides intensive counseling, education and support services to young girls and women who are parents, many of whom have a history of substance abuse. The Program helps women to remain drug free; develop appropriate parenting and other life skills; and to become regularly engaged in constructive activities that promote positive family and community lifestyles.

Many of the women and young girls who are served by the Family Services Center have a background of public assistance. Some are single parents, some are married, and some have steady work histories. What all of these women have in common is that they have been overwhelmed by the pressures and destructive influences of an environment and culture where substance abuse and crime run rampant, and poverty and dependence are a way of life. Mind-Builders Family Services Center offers at-risk families a real alternative with practical help available 24 hours a day.

Mind-Builders has a continuous record of honest and effective service based on the premise that communities can best respond to the urban crisis by drawing upon their own traditions, talents and determination to create positive alternatives for families. With the Family Services Center, Mind-Builders further enhances a community movement, thus enabling a neighborhood to achieve empowerment and act as a positive force for change.

Our project budget for this year is $358,281. To date, we have secured a $300,000 lead grant from the Child Welfare Administration and have received one generous commitment of $25,000 for this project from the Alternative Trust. To meet our budget, we must raise $33,281 from the private sector. We request a grant of $10,000 from the Good Works Foundation to help maintain the Family Service Center's counseling and support services offered to at-risk women and girls.

STATEMENT OF NEED

Mind-Builders serves the communities of Williamsbridge-Wakefield. Both neighborhoods are fragile places with uncertain futures. Poverty, crime and drug use have increased at an alarming rate in this area over the past 20 years. Working class families struggle to maintain a good quality of life within this economically mixed area set against a backdrop of major areas of poverty and significant crime. Because of their critical importance, New York City has designated these neighborhoods as Special Neighborhood Stabilization Areas and targeted them as a priority for human service resources. Mind-Builders is the only organization of its kind in an area underserved by social programs and youth services.

The young women and girls of our community face an enormous uphill struggle to make a safe passage through adolescence into adulthood. As teenagers, they are often overwhelmed by the difficulties of living in a hostile environment where widespread drug use and street violence and crime put personal safety at constant risk.

The very common occurrence of teenage pregnancy, combined with a lack of economic resources and employable skills have put many young women on a fast track to welfare dependency before they have even left their teens. Most recent statistics for our community show that 41.5% of our young people 18 years and under reside in households dependent on public assistance.

Young women too often adopt behavior patterned on a cycle of poverty and dependence. These women grow up resisting and fearing change from the habits they have picked up on the streets, which often includes alcohol and/or substance abuse.

The economic and social pressures faced by young women and girls who have children stretches families to the breaking point. When mothers turn to alcohol and/or substance abuse, or succumb to other pressures, the family falls apart, and the children are placed in foster care. The costs to society, in both human and monetary terms, resulting from the separation of children from their families are tremendous. To avoid these devastating losses we must respond by empowering, not punishing young girls and women and helping them to build positive lifestyles and to maintain their families.

PROGRAM DESCRIPTION

Goals and Objectives

The goal of Mind-Builders Family Services Center is to help young women and girls overcome patterns of substance abuse and other destructive influences and to avoid the placement of children in foster care. The objective of the program is to improve the living situation of these families by using a holistic and grass-roots approach to promote self-sufficiency. Through this program, we seek integration of independent, successful families back into the community where they may establish and pursue productive lives.

Background

The Family Services Center established at Mind-Builders in 1992 is a restoration of a New York State demonstration model successfully piloted by Mind-Builders from 1988-1990. Like the earlier project, services are designed around a core counseling program in which three case workers serve 30 to 40 high risk girls and women a year, and their families, in an intensive effort to stabilize their lives in the community and to avoid family breakup or foster care placement.

The Family Services Center is centrally located within our service community of Williamsbridge-Wakefield and operates out of an inviting storefront located a short walking distance from the Mind-Builders main building. In addition to providing counseling, the Center serves as an information resource for women, girls, and other community residents who may drop in for literature and/or referrals to other community resources.

Program Enrollment

Mind-Builders Family Services Center serves young women and girls whose families are at risk of breakdown or separation. Many of the women and girls are referred to the program by the Child Welfare Administration's Field Service staff after voluntary application for child abuse/neglect prevention services. Some of the women come to the Family Services Center having been referred by personnel of local schools, hospitals, other social institutions and community organizations. Mind-Builders staff make referrals to the Family Services Center for parents of children enrolled in other Mind-Builders activities. Other women and girls are drawn to the Center by word of mouth, or independently decide to drop in to use the social information center, obtain program help, or obtain related information and/or referrals to other community resources.

Caseloads are kept small with maximum enrollment for the program set at 40 girls and women each year. This cap, based on prior program experience, ensures that our staff is able to provide an intensive, caring and cost efficient alternative to foster care services.

Program Design and Implementation

The Family Services Center establishes a supportive, task-centered and goal oriented partnership with the families. The Center combines intensive counseling, 24-hour crisis intervention by beeper, and the development of life and parenting skills. The Center arranges for training, advocacy, supplemental child care, nutrition and health care education and transportation and/or escort services that enable families to stay together in their communities.

Within 48 hours of referral from a Child Welfare Administration worker, a Family Center Counselor completes a joint visit with the CWA worker to the family's home for a formal introduction to the family. The Family Services Center Staff are expected to perform whatever tasks are reasonable and necessary to ensure the safety of the mothers and children in their own home, while exhausting every effort to prevent the children's foster care placement. Staff Counselors develop trusting and supportive relationships with the women and girls and their children. Counselors assess, identify and reassess family problems; develop prioritized strategies for the problems' resolution; and structure plans to accomplish their goals.

In addition, a series of Family Education Workshops presents speakers who discuss issues and topics of relevance to women. Presentations scheduled for this year include; "Family Conflicts—Problem Resolution and Effective Communication," "Parenting Skills—Discipline and Praise/Constructive Criticism and Building Self-Esteem in Children," and "Job Readiness and Family Budgeting—Earning an Income and Making the Most of It."

EVALUATION

The Family Services Center staff meet weekly to discuss and evaluate individual cases and share ideas to develop and execute plans to serve the program participants' needs. A Staff Survey and a Family Interview Questionnaire are completed after the six month interval of each family's involvement in the program. Pursuant to a CWA mandate the program must provide monthly statistical reports and schedule periodic on-site visits.

Mind-Builders is in the process of structuring a formal Family Services Center evaluation component for integration into routine service operation. The new evaluation component will consist of an evaluation by an independent source, program audits and/or review of program planning and management systems.

ORGANIZATION INFORMATION

Founded in 1978, Mind-Builders has grown from a small neighborhood program serving 40 children, to a multi-service agency offering professional instruction in music, dance and theater, as well as cultural and educational programs and counseling to more than 1,000 young people and their families. The agency is located in and serves the Northeast Bronx communities of Williamsbridge and Wakefield. The ethnic composition of our service community is 64% African American, 26% Latino and 10% White.

Mind-Builders' programs are widely recognized for their innovative approaches to the development of literacy, cultural awareness and academic achievement that empower young people to effect positive change and growth. Our educational programs and intensive arts instruction help youngsters unlock and develop qualities essential to success—inspiration, discipline, creativity and motivation. Most of our students are ages eight through 15, but many pre-schoolers and adults also participate in agency programs and activities.

CONCLUSION

As a service leader for our community, Mind-Builders is well positioned to attract young women who so desperately need help in facing tremendous life challenges that threaten to tear their families apart. Mind-Builders Family Services Center is a timely and creative response to those social conditions that threaten the stability of our families and children.

To continue this valuable program, we need the financial support and partnership of funders like the Good Works Foundation. A grant from the Good Works Foundation is an investment in the lives of young women in Williamsbridge and Wakefield. The result: a healthy environment for their children and a better future for our community.

PROGRAM BUDGET

EXPENSES

Personnel

Executive Director (20% of full-time expense)	$ 13,200
Executive Assistant (20% of full-time expense)	7,200
Program Coordinator (20% of full-time expense)	9,600
Development Coordinator (20% of full-time expense)	3,000
Bookkeeper (20% of full-time expense)	7,800
Payroll Clerk (20% of full-time expense)	3,600
Custodian (20% of full-time expense)	3,600
Accountant (20% of full-time expense)	8,100
Receptionist (20% of full-time expense)	2,030
Director of Family Services (100% of full-time expense)	42,000
Family Services Center Counselors (3 at 100% of full-time expense)	81,000
Family Services Center Assistants (2 at 100% of full-time expense)	42,000
Subtotal	$223,130
Fringe Benefits (24%)	53,551
Consultants	1,050
Total Personnel Expense	$277,731

Non-Personnel

Rent/Space Costs	$ 24,600
Equipment	9,110
General Operating Costs (e.g. postage, electricity, telephone, travel, supplies, printing)	42,700
Miscellaneous	4,140
Total Non-Personnel Expense	$ 80,550
Total Expense	**$358,281**

APPENDIX C

Selected Readings on Proposal Development

Compiled by Jean Johnson and Sarah Collins

Especially recommended for the novice grantseeker:

Brooklyn In Touch Information Center. *Fundraising with Proposals.*
Brooklyn, NY (1 Hanson Pl., Room 2504, 11243): Brooklyn In Touch
Information Center, 1988. 13 p.

> Basic guide for the novice fundraiser. Includes an introduc-
> tory article—"How to Know Your Grantmaker"—on how
> to begin research on funding sources, tables, lists of fund-
> raising turnoffs, as well as a sample proposal outline and a
> cover letter.

Browning, Beverly A. *Successful Grant Writing Tips: The Manual.*
Burton, MI (4355 South Saginaw Street, 48529): Grantsline Inc.,
1991. iii, 91 p.

> Covers each element of a proposal, complete with exam-
> ples, tables, and graphics.

Burns, Michael E. *Proposal Writer's Guide.* New Haven, CT (70 Audubon St., 06510): D.A.T.A., 1993. 57 p.
> Step-by-step approach to preparing written funding requests. Includes four sample proposals.

Kiritz, Norton J. *Program Planning and Proposal Writing: Expanded Version.* Grantsmanship Center Reprint Series on Program Planning & Proposal Writing. Los Angeles, CA (1125 W. 6th St., 90017): Grantsmanship Center, 1980. 47 p.
> Step-by-step guide to a widely used format in clear, concise language.

Zimmerman, Robert M., and Ann W. Lehman. *Grant Writing and Fundraising Fundamentals.* San Francisco, CA (582 Market Street, Suite 112, 94104): Zimmerman, Lehman & Associates, 1993. 51 p.
> Basic guide that covers researching possible grants, proposal writing, direct mail solicitation, special events, and planned giving. Includes a sample proposal.

For more advanced fundraisers:

Belcher, Jane C., and Julia M. Jacobsen. *From Idea to Funded Project: Grant Proposals that Work.* 4th ed., rev. Phoenix, AZ. (2214 North Central, 85004-1483): Oryx Press, 1992. v, 138 p.
> Presents a method for nurturing an idea from inception through the process of developing a proposal, finding sources of support, administering grants, and evaluation. Second part provides information on basic resources and reprints several forms and regulations for government funding sources.

Bowman, Joel P., and Bernardine P. Branchaw. *How to Write Proposals that Produce.* Phoenix, AZ (2214 North Central, 85004-1483): Oryx Press, 1992. xii, 236 p.
> Detailed and technical treatment of the process of writing proposals. Geared toward both business and nonprofit organizations.

Carlson, Mim. *Winning Grants Step by Step: Support Centers of America's Complete Workbook for Planning, Developing and Writing Successful Proposals.* The Jossey-Bass Nonprofit Sector Series. San Francisco, CA (350 Sansome Street, 94104): Jossey-Bass, 1995. xi, 115 p.

> Contains exercises designed to help with proposal planning, proposal writing, and meeting the requirements of both government agencies and private funders. A resource section gives tips on how to research funders, write a letter of intent, and evaluate a proposal through the funder's eyes. Includes a bibliography.

Coley, Soraya M., and Cynthia A. Scheinberg. *Proposal Writing.* Sage Human Services Guides, no. 63. Newbury Park, CA (2455 Teller Road, 91320): Sage Publications, 1990. 130 p.

> Intended primarily for the moderately experienced grant-seeker, this guide provides step-by-step advice for developing proposals. Examples and worksheets throughout.

Frost, Gordon Jay. *Winning Grant Proposals: Eleven Successful Appeals by American Nonprofits to Corporations, Foundations, Individuals, and Government Agencies.* Rockville, MD (12300 Twinbrook Parkway, Suite 450, 20852): Fund Raising Institute, 1993. ii, 160 p.

> Collects a group of funded proposals with amounts granted ranging from five thousand to one million dollars. Several proposals include cover letters; most include budgets.

Gooch, Judith Mirick. *Writing Winning Proposals.* Washington, DC (11 Dupont Circle, Suite 400, 20036): Council for Advancement and Support of Education, 1987. vii, 87 p.

> Focuses primarily on college and university proposal writing, but provides general information useful to all grant-seekers. Detailed—includes a case study, samples, and a bibliography.

Hale, Phale D., Jr. *Writing Grant Proposals That Win!* Alexandria, VA (1101 King Street, P.O. Box 1453, 22313-2053): Capitol Publications, 1992. 147 p.

> Covers the major elements of any proposal. Also discusses the difference between responding to federal requests-for-proposals and applying to private funders, writing for the reviewer, and the politics of proposal writing. Includes a sample proposal.

Hall, Mary S. *Getting Funded: A Complete Guide to Proposal Writing.* 3rd ed. Portland, OR (P.O. Box 1491, 97207): Continuing Education Press, 1988. viii, 206 p.

> This soup-to-nuts guidebook is organized in a logical planning pattern. Each chapter of the section dealing with the actual writing of a proposal focuses on a specific component. Includes resource lists, cases, models, checklists, and sample formats.

Lefferts, Robert B. *Getting a Grant in the 1990s: How to Write Successful Grant Proposals.* New York, NY (15 Columbus Circle, 10023): Prentice Hall Press, 1990. xiii, 239 p.

> Manual provides guidelines for preparing, writing, and presenting proposals to foundations and government agencies. Intended for those seeking funding for human services. Includes a critiqued sample program proposal, a glossary, and annotated bibliographies.

Meador, Roy. *Guidelines for Preparing Proposals.* 2nd ed. Chelsea, MI (121 South Main Street, 48118): Lewis Publishers, 1991. xiii, 204 p.

> Advanced manual on proposals for corporations, government, and foundations. The book contains standard guidelines for a proposal but with the additional guidelines necessary for use for a highly technical or scientific project.

APPENDIX D

Publications and Services of the Foundation Center

The Foundation Center is a national service organization founded and supported by foundations to provide a single authoritative source of information on foundation and corporate giving. The Center's programs are designed to help grantseekers select those funders which may be most interested in their projects from the more than 40,000 active U.S. foundations. Among its primary activities toward this end are publishing reference books and CD-ROMs on foundation and corporate philanthropy and disseminating information on grant-making through a nationwide public service program.

The Foundation Center's publications and electronic resources are the primary working tools of every serious grantseeker. They are also used by grantmakers, scholars, journalists, and legislators—in short, by anyone seeking any type of factual information on philanthropy. All private foundations and a significant number of corporations actively engaged in grantmaking, regardless of size or geographic location, are included in one or more of the Center's publications. The publications are of three kinds: directories that describe specific funders, characterizing their program interests and providing fiscal and personnel data; grants indexes that list and classify by subject recent foundation and corporate awards; and guides, monographs, and bibliographies that introduce the reader to funding research, elements of proposal writing, and nonprofit management issues. The Center's full database of more than 40,000 foundations and corporate givers and their associated grants is also available in a searchable CD-ROM format.

Foundation Center publications and CD-ROMs may be ordered from the Foundation Center, 79 Fifth Avenue, New York, NY 10003-3076. For more information about any aspect of the Center's program or for the name of the Center's library collection nearest you, call 1-800-424-9836, or visit our World Wide Web site at http://fdncenter.org.

GENERAL RESEARCH DIRECTORIES

THE FOUNDATION DIRECTORY, 1997 Edition

The Foundation Directory includes the latest information on all foundations whose assets exceed $2 million or whose annual grants total $200,000 or more. The 1997 Edition includes more than 7,700 of these foundations, over 500 of which are new to this edition. *Directory* foundations hold more than $170 billion in assets and award $10 billion in grants annually, accounting for 90 percent of all U.S. foundation dollars awarded in 1995.

Each *Directory* entry contains precise information on application procedures, giving limitations, types of support awarded, the publications of each foundation, and foundation staff. In addition, each entry features such data as the grantmaker's giving interests, financial data, grant amounts, address, and telephone number. This edition includes over 38,000 selected grants. The Foundation Center works closely with foundations to ensure the accuracy and timeliness of the information provided.

The *Directory* includes indexes by foundation name; subject areas of interest; names of donors, officers, and trustees; geographic location; international interests; and types of support awarded. Also included are analyses of the foundation community by geography, asset and grant size, and the different foundation types.

March 1997
Softbound: ISBN 0-87954-706-5 / $190
Hardbound: ISBN 0-87954-705-7 / $215   *Published annually*

THE FOUNDATION DIRECTORY PART 2, 1997

The Foundation Directory Part 2 has the same coverage for the next largest set of foundations, those whose assets range from $1 million to $2 million or grant programs from $50,000 to $200,000. It includes *Directory*-level information on mid-sized foundations. Data on over 4,500 foundations is included along with more than 20,000 recently awarded foundation grants. Access to foundation entries is facilitated by six indexes, including foundation name; subject areas of interest; names of donors, officers, and trustees; geographic location; international interests; and types of support awarded.

March 1997 / ISBN 0-87954-708-1 / $185   *Published annually*

THE FOUNDATION DIRECTORY SUPPLEMENT

The Foundation Directory Supplement provides information on *Foundation Directory* and *Foundation Directory Part 2* grantmakers six months after those volumes are published. The *Supplement* ensures that users of the *Directory* and *Directory Part 2* have the latest addresses, contact names, policy statements, application guidelines, and financial data for foundations.

September 1997 / ISBN 0-87954-720-0 / $135   *Published annually*

GUIDE TO U.S. FOUNDATIONS, THEIR TRUSTEES, OFFICERS, AND DONORS, 1997 Edition

This reference tool provides current, accurate information on more than 38,800 private grantmaking foundations in the U.S. The two-volume set also includes a master list of the names of the people who establish, oversee, and manage those institutions. Each entry includes asset and giving amounts as well as geographic limitations.

The *Guide to U.S. Foundations* is the only source of published data on thousands of local foundations. (It includes more than 26,000 grantmakers not covered in other Foundation Center publications.) Each entry also tells you whether you can find more extensive information on the grantmaker in another Foundation Center reference work.

April 1997 / 0-87954-707-3 / $225   *Published annually*

THE FOUNDATION 1000

The Foundation 1000 provides access to extensive and accurate information on the 1,000 largest foundations in the country, a group of grantmakers responsible for distributing more than 65 percent of all foundation grant dollars. *Foundation 1000* grantmakers hold over $139 billion in assets and each year award more than 210,000 grants worth nearly $7 billion to nonprofit organizations nationwide.

The Foundation 1000 provides the most thorough analyses available. Each multipage foundation profile features a full foundation portrait, a detailed breakdown of the foundation's grant programs, and extensive lists of recently awarded foundation grants.

Five indexes help target potential funders in a variety of ways: by subject field, type of support, geographic location, international giving, and the names of foundation officers, donors, and trustees.

November 1996 / ISBN 0-87954-665-4 / $295   *Published annually*

NATIONAL DIRECTORY OF CORPORATE GIVING, 4th Edition

The 4th Edition of the *National Directory of Corporate Giving* offers authoritative information on more than 2,600 corporate foundations and direct-giving programs.

This volume features detailed portraits of 1,972 corporate foundations plus an additional 670 direct-giving programs, including application information, key personnel, types of support generally awarded, giving limitations, financial data, and purpose and activities statements. Also included are more than 9,900 selected grants. The volume also provides data on the corporations that sponsor foundations and on direct-giving programs. Each entry gives the company's name and address, a listing of its types of business, its financial data (with *Forbes* and *Fortune* ratings), a listing of its subsidiaries, divisions, plants, and offices and a charitable-giving statement.

The *National Directory of Corporate Giving* also features an extensive bibliography. Six indexes help target funding prospects by geographic region; types of support; subject area; officers, donors, and trustees; types of business; and the names of the corporation, its foundation, and its direct-giving program.

October 1995 / ISBN 0-87954-646-8 / $195   *Published biennially*

CORPORATE FOUNDATION PROFILES, 9th Edition

This biennial volume includes comprehensive information on 235 of the largest corporate foundations in the U.S., grantmakers who each give at least $1.25 million annually. Each profile includes foundation giving interests, application guidelines, recently awarded grants, information on the sponsoring company, and other fundraising facts. A section on financial data provides a summary of the size and grantmaking capacity of each foundation and contains a list of assets, gifts or contributions, grants paid, operating programs, expenditures, scholarships, and loans. An appendix lists core financial data on some 1,200 additional corporate foundations, all of which give at least $50,000 in grants every year. Three indexes help grantseekers search for prospective funders by subject area, geographic region, and types of support favored by the foundation.

February 1996 / ISBN 0-87954-653-0 / $155   *Published biennially*

NATIONAL DIRECTORY OF GRANTMAKING PUBLIC CHARITIES, 1st Edition

The 1st Edition of this volume features current information on more than 800 public charities—grantmakers that, up to now, have been difficult to locate or have been simply overlooked. This directory includes 450 community foundations, all of which offer some form of financial support to nonprofit organizations or individuals, whether it be grants, scholarships, fellowships,

198

loans, or in-kind gifts. It includes descriptions of more than 1,200 selected grants, which often provide the best indication of giving interests, and indexes by subject interest, types of support, geographic preferences, and names of officers and trustees.

November 1995 / ISBN 0-87954-651-4 / $95

GUIDE TO GREATER WASHINGTON D.C. GRANTMAKERS, 2nd Edition

The *Guide to Greater Washington D.C. Grantmakers* provides current, accurate data on more than 1,000 area grantmakers—foundations, corporate giving programs, and public charities. Each grantmaker portrait includes an application address, financial data, giving limitations, and the names of key officials. For larger foundations—those that give at least $50,000 in grants annually—application procedures and giving interest statements are also provided. In addition, there are more than 1,800 descriptions of recently awarded grants.

July 1996 / ISBN 0-87954-664-6 / $60

NEW YORK STATE FOUNDATIONS: A Comprehensive Directory, 5th Edition

New York State Foundations offers complete coverage of more than 5,500 independent, corporate, and community foundations throughout New York State. Many entries include descriptions of recently awarded grants. A separate section covers hundreds of out-of-state grantmakers that fund nonprofits in New York State. Six indexes offer quick access to foundations by fields of interest; international interests; types of support awarded; city and county; names of donors, officers, and trustees; and foundation names.

May 1997 / ISBN 0-87954-717-0 / $180   *Published biennially*

DIRECTORY OF MISSOURI GRANTMAKERS, 1st Edition

The *Directory of Missouri Grantmakers* provides a comprehensive guide to grantmakers in the state—over 800 foundations, corporate giving programs, and public charities. Entries list giving amounts, fields of interest, purpose statements, selected grants, and more. Indexes help target the most appropriate funders by subject interest, types of support, and names of key personnel.

June 1995 / ISBN 0-87954-612-3 / $75

FOUNDATION GRANTS TO INDIVIDUALS, 10th Edition

The 10th Edition of this volume features more than 3,300 entries, all of which profile foundation grants to individuals. Entries include foundation addresses and telephone numbers, financial data, giving limitations, and application guidelines.

May 1997 / ISBN 0-87954-713-8 / $65   *Published biennially*

SUBJECT DIRECTORIES

The Foundation Center's National Guide to Funding series is designed to facilitate grantseeking within specific fields. Each of the directories described below identifies a set of grantmakers that have already stated or demonstrated an interest in a particular field. Entries provide access to foundation addresses, financial data, giving priorities, application procedures, contact names, and key officials. Many entries also feature recently awarded grants. A variety of indexes help fundraisers target potential grant sources by subject area, geographic preferences, types of support, and the names of donors, officers, and trustees.

AIDS FUNDING: A Guide to Giving by Foundations and Charitable Organizations, 4th Edition

This volume covers more than 600 foundations, corporate giving programs, and public charities that support AIDS- and HIV-related nonprofit organizations involved in direct relief, medical research, legal aid, preventative education, and other programs to empower persons with AIDS and AIDS-related diseases. Grants lists showing the types of projects funded by grantmakers accompany 312 entries.
December 1995 / ISBN 0-87954-647-6 / $75

GUIDE TO FUNDING FOR INTERNATIONAL AND FOREIGN PROGRAMS, 3rd Edition

The 3rd Edition of this guide covers over 700 foundations and corporate direct-giving programs interested in funding projects with an international focus, both within the U.S. and abroad. Program areas include international relief, disaster assistance, human rights, civil liberties, community development, education, and more. The volume also includes descriptions of more than 6,000 recently awarded grants.
May 1996 / ISBN 0-87954-657-3 / $115

FUNDING IN AGING: A Guide to Giving by Foundations, Corporations, and Charitable Organizations

Funding in Aging provides essential facts on more than 1,000 grantmakers with a specific interest in the field of aging. This guide includes addresses, financial data, giving priorities, application procedures, contact names, and key officials. The volume also provides recent grants lists with descriptions of more than 1,000 grants for over 300 foundation entries. Section II includes basic descriptions and contact information for nearly 100 voluntary organizations that offer technical assistance or information to older Americans and the agencies that serve them.
October 1996 / ISBN 0-87954-663-8 / $95

NATIONAL GUIDE TO FUNDING IN ARTS AND CULTURE, 4th Edition

The 4th Edition of this volume covers more than 4,000 grantmakers with an interest in funding art colonies, dance companies, museums, theaters, and

other types of arts and cultural projects and institutions. The volume also includes more than 11,000 descriptions of recently awarded grants.
June 1996 / ISBN 0-87954-660-3 / $145

NATIONAL GUIDE TO FUNDING FOR CHILDREN, YOUTH AND FAMILIES, 4th Edition

This guide provides facts on some 3,400 foundations and corporate direct-giving programs that together award millions of dollars each year to organizations committed to causes involving children, youth, and families. Each entry includes the grantmaker's address and contact person, purpose statement, and application guidelines. There are also descriptions of more than 13,000 sample grants recently awarded by many of these foundations.
April 1997 / ISBN 0-87954-711-1 / $150

NATIONAL GUIDE TO FUNDING FOR COMMUNITY DEVELOPMENT, 1st Edition

This guide contains facts on more than 2,500 foundations and corporate direct-giving progams. Entries feature: address and contact names, giving interest statements, current financial data, key personnel, application guidelines, and more than 8,000 descriptions of recently awarded grants. There are three indexes: subject field, geographic area, and type of support.
May 1996 / ISBN 0-87954-659-X / $135

NATIONAL GUIDE TO FUNDING FOR ELEMENTARY AND SECONDARY EDUCATION, 4th Edition

This volume has information on more than 2,000 foundations and corporate giving programs that support nursery schools, bilingual education initiatives, remedial reading/math programs, drop-out prevention services, educational testing programs, and many other nonprofit organizations and initiatives. The volume also includes descriptions of nearly 6,400 recently awarded grants.
May 1997 / ISBN 0-87954-715-4 / $140

NATIONAL GUIDE TO FUNDING FOR INFORMATION TECHNOLOGY, 1st Edition

This new guide provides facts on more than 800 foundations and corporate direct giving programs that award grants to projects involving information technology. The guide also includes descriptions of more than 10,000 recently awarded grants for computer science, engineering and technology, telecommunications, and media and communications.
May 1997 / ISBN 0-87954-709-X / $115

NATIONAL GUIDE TO FUNDING FOR THE ENVIRONMENT AND ANIMAL WELFARE, 3rd Edition

The 3rd Edition of this guide covers over 1,700 foundations and corporate direct-giving programs that fund nonprofits involved in international conservation, ecological research, waste reduction, animal welfare, and more. The volume includes descriptions of more than 4,000 recently awarded grants.

May 1996 / ISBN 0-87954-662-X / $95

NATIONAL GUIDE TO FUNDING IN HEALTH, 5th Edition

The 5th Edition of this guide contains facts on more than 3,400 foundations and corporate direct-giving programs interested in funding hospitals, universities, research institutes, community-based agencies, national health associations, and a broad range of other health-related programs and services. The volume also includes descriptions of more than 13,800 recently awarded grants.

April 1997 / ISBN 0-87954-710-3 / $150

NATIONAL GUIDE TO FUNDING IN HIGHER EDUCATION, 4th Edition

The 4th Edition of this guide includes information on more than 4,500 grant-makers with an interest in funding colleges, universities, graduate programs, and research institutes, as well as descriptions of more than 15,000 recently awarded grants.

June 1996 / ISBN 0-87954-661-1 / $145

NATIONAL GUIDE TO FUNDING FOR LIBRARIES AND INFORMATION SERVICES, 4th Edition

This guide provides data on more than 600 foundations and corporate direct-giving programs that support a wide range of organizations and initiatives, from the smallest public libraries to major research institutions, academic/research libraries, art, law, and medical libraries, and other specialized information centers. The volume also includes descriptions of more than 1,000 recently awarded grants.

April 1997 / ISBN 0-87954-716-2 / $95

NATIONAL GUIDE TO FUNDING IN RELIGION, 4th Edition

The 3rd Edition of this guide provides access to information on more than 4,200 foundations and corporate direct-giving programs that have demonstrated or stated an interest in funding churches, missionary societies, religious welfare and education programs, and many other types of projects and institutions. The volume also includes descriptions of more than 5,300 recently awarded grants.

April 1997 / ISBN 0-87954-714-6 / $140

NATIONAL GUIDE TO FUNDING IN SUBSTANCE ABUSE, 1st Edition

The guide contains facts on more than 600 foundations and corporate direct-giving programs interested in funding counseling services, preventive education, treatment, medical research, residential care and halfway houses, and projects addressing alcohol and drug abuse, smoking addiction, and drunk driving. The volume also includes descriptions of some 695 recently awarded grants.

April 1995 / ISBN 0-87954-602-6 / $95

NATIONAL GUIDE TO FUNDING FOR WOMEN AND GIRLS, 4th Edition

The 4th Edition of this guide covers some 1,000 foundations and corporate direct-giving programs with an interest in funding such projects as education scholarships, shelters for abused women, girls' clubs, health clinics, employment centers, and other programs. The volume also provides descriptions of more than 4,000 recently awarded grants.

May 1997 / ISBN 0-87954-712-X / $115

GRANT DIRECTORIES

GRANT GUIDES

This series of guides lists actual foundation grants of $10,000 or more in 31 key areas.

Each title in the series affords access to the names, addresses, and giving limitations of the foundations listed. The grant descriptions provide the grant recipient's name and location; the amount of the grant; the date the grant was authorized; and a description of the grant's intended use.

Each *Grant Guide* includes three indexes: the type of organization generally funded by the grantmaker, the subject focus of the foundation's grants, and the geographic area in which the foundation has already funded projects.

Each *Grant Guide*'s introduction presents a series of statistical tables to document such findings as (1) the 25 top funders in a given area of interest; (2) the 15 largest grants reported; (3) the total dollar amount and number of grants awarded for specific types of support, recipient organization type, and population group; and (4) the total grant dollars received in each U.S. state and in many foreign countries.

Series published annually in October / 1996 Editions / $75 each

THE FOUNDATION GRANTS INDEX, 1997 Edition

The 1997 (25th) Edition of *The Foundation Grants Index* covers the grantmaking programs of more than 1,000 of the largest independent, corporate, and community foundations in the U.S. and includes more than 73,000 grant descriptions.

Grant descriptions are divided into 28 broad subject areas such as health, higher education, and arts and culture. Within each of these broad fields, the grant descriptions are listed geographically by state and alphabetically by the name of the foundation.

November 1996/ ISBN 0-87954-701-4 / $160   *Published annually*

THE FOUNDATION GRANTS INDEX QUARTERLY

This subscription service provides up-to-date information on foundation funding every three months. Each issue delivers descriptions of more than 5,000 recent foundation grants, arranged by state and indexed by subject and recipient. The *Quarterly* also notes changes in foundation address, personnel, program interests, and application procedures, as well as a list of grantmakers' recent publications such as annual reports, information brochures, grants lists, and newsletters.
Annual subscription $95 / 4 issues ISSN 0735-2522

WHO GETS GRANTS: Foundation Grants to Nonprofit Organizations, 4th Edition

Who Gets Grants provides direct access to grant recipient information on more than 32,000 nonprofit organizations and more than 73,000 grants.

Because the book is divided into 19 different subject headings, fundraisers can scan through grants recently awarded within their field to generate lists of grant prospects. Within each subject area the grant recipients are listed by geographic area.

The grant recipient entries feature grant descriptions that include the grant amount, its duration and use, and the name of the grantmaker, while an index lists all the grants made by each foundation covered.
February 1997 / ISBN 0-87954-704-9 / $135

GUIDEBOOKS, MANUALS, AND REPORTS

AIDS FUNDRAISING

Published in conjunction with Funders Concerned About AIDS, *AIDS Fundraising* covers an array of money-generating initiatives, from membership drives to special events and direct mail.
July 1991 / ISBN 0-87954-390-6 / $10

ARTS FUNDING

This study, commissioned by Grantmakers in the Arts, provides a framework for understanding recent trends in foundation funding for arts and culture. The report analyzes grants awarded in the 1980s and also includes profiles of more than 60 top foundation and corporate grantmakers in the arts.
April 1993 / ISBN 0-87594-448-1 / $40

ARTS FUNDING REVISITED

Arts Funding Revisited focuses on grantmaking in 1992, updating the original study by three years. It analyzes more than 9,500 grants awarded in that year by over 800 of the major U.S. arts and culture grantmakers, providing a current picture of giving priorities in the field.
July 1995 / ISBN 0-87594-650-6 / $14.95

THE FOUNDATION CENTER'S GRANTS CLASSIFICATION SYSTEM INDEXING MANUAL WITH THESAURUS, Revised Edition

The *Grants Classification Manual* includes a complete set of classification codes to facilitate precise tracking of grants and recipients by subject, recipient type, and population categories. It also features a revised thesaurus to help identify the "official" terms and codes that represent thousands of subject areas and recipient types in the Center's system of grants classification.
May 1995 / ISBN 0-87954-644-1 / $95

FOUNDATION FUNDAMENTALS: A Guide for Grantseekers, 5th Edition

This comprehensive guidebook takes you step-by-step through the funding research process. Worksheets and checklists are provided. Comprehensive bibliographies, detailed research examples, and an index are also supplied.
June 1994 / ISBN 0-87954-543-7 / $24.95

THE FOUNDATION CENTER'S USER-FRIENDLY GUIDE: A Grantseeker's Guide to Resources, 4th Edition

This book answers the most commonly asked questions about grantseeking. Specifically designed for novice grantseekers, the *User-Friendly Guide* leads the reader through the unfamiliar jargon and wide range of print and electronic resources used by professional fundraisers.
July 1996 / ISBN 0-87954-666-2 / $14.95

FOUNDATION GIVING: Yearbook of Facts and Figures on Private, Corporate and Community Foundations, 1996 Edition

Foundation Giving provides a comprehensive overview of the latest trends in foundation giving in the U.S. This volume uses a range of statistical tables to chart foundation giving by subject area and type of support, to categorize foundations by asset and giving amount, and to document other data such as the breakdown of grants awarded by the 100 largest foundations.
July 1996 / ISBN 0-87954-667-0 / $24.95

PROGRAM-RELATED INVESTMENTS: A GUIDE TO FUNDERS AND TRENDS

PRIs are alternative financing approaches for supplying capital to the nonprofit sector. This type of investment has been used to support community revitalization, low-income housing, microenterprise development, historic preservation, human services, and more.

The Foundation Center's *Program-Related Investments: A Guide to Funders and Trends* offers information on this little-understood field, including current perspectives from providers and recipients; essays by experts in the field; strategies for success; and a directory of more than 100 leading PRI providers.
April 1995 / ISBN 0-87954-558-5 / $45

BIBLIOGRAPHIES

THE LITERATURE OF THE NONPROFIT SECTOR: A Bibliography with Abstracts, Volumes 1–8

This bibliographical series lists references on fundraising, foundations, corporate giving, nonprofit management, and more, many with abstracts. Each volume is divided into 12 broad subject fields and includes a subject, title, and author index. The 8th volume expands series coverage to more than 14,000 titles.

Volume 8, December 1996 / ISBN 0-87954-702-2 / $45
Volume 7, December 1995 / ISBN 0-87954-649-2 / $45
Volume 6, December 1994 / ISBN 0-87954-561-5 / $45
Volume 5, November 1993 / ISBN 0-87954-509-7 / $45
Volume 4, September 1992 / ISBN 0-87954-447-3 / $45
Volume 3, September 1991 / ISBN 0-87954-386-8 / $45
Volume 2, July 1990 / ISBN 0-87954-343-4 / $45
Volume 1, August 1989 / ISBN 0-87954-287-X / $55
Volumes 1–8 Set / $255

OTHER PUBLICATIONS

AMERICA'S NONPROFIT SECTOR: A Primer

by Lester M. Salamon

Illustrated with numerous charts and tables that explain various aspects of the nonprofit world, this book is an easy-to-understand primer for anyone who wants to comprehend the makeup of America's nonprofit sector.

August 1992 / ISBN 0-87954-451-1 / $14.95

BEST PRACTICES OF EFFECTIVE NONPROFIT ORGANIZATIONS: A Practitioner's Manual

By Philip Berstein

Philip Bernstein has drawn on his own extensive experience as a nonprofit executive, consultant and volunteer to produce this review of "best practices" adopted by successful nonprofit organizations. Topics covered include defining purposes and goals, creating comprehensive financing plans, evaluating services, and effective communication.

January 1997 / ISBN 0-87954-755-3 / $29.95

THE BOARD MEMBER'S BOOK, 2nd Edition

by Brian O'Connell, President-Emeritus, INDEPENDENT SECTOR

Based on his extensive experience working with and on the boards of voluntary organizations, Brian O'Connell has developed this practical guide to the essential functions of voluntary boards. O'Connell offers practical advice on how to be a more effective board member as well as on how board members can help their organizations make a difference, and also provides an extensive reading list.

October 1993 / ISBN 0-87954-502-X / $24.95

CAREERS FOR DREAMERS AND DOERS: A Guide to Management Careers in the Nonprofit Sector

by Lilly Cohen and Dennis R.Young

Careers for Dreamers and Doers offers practical advice for starting a job search and suggests strategies used by successful managers throughout the voluntary sector. The book draws from experience of established professionals, providing career histories of nonprofit CEOs, development officers, and foundation officials. It also covers compensation patterns in the field, the fundamentals of resume writing and interviewing, and nonprofit management programs at colleges and universities.

November 1989 / ISBN 0-87954-294-2 / $24.95

ECONOMICS FOR NONPROFIT MANAGERS

by Dennis R. Young and Richard Steinberg

Young and Steinberg introduce and explain concepts such as opportunity cost, analysis at the margin, market equilibrium, market failure, and cost-benefit analysis. This volume also focuses on issues of particular concern to nonprofits, such as the economics of fundraising and volunteer recruiting, the regulatory environment, the impact of competition on nonprofit performance, interactions among sources of revenue, and more.

July 1995 / ISBN 0-87954-610-7 / $34.95

HANDBOOK ON PRIVATE FOUNDATIONS

by David F. Freeman and the Council on Foundations

In this revised edition, sponsored by the Council on Foundations, author David F. Freeman offers advice on establishing, staffing, and governing foundations and provides insights into legal and tax guidelines as well. Each chapter concludes with a useful annotated bibliography.

September 1991
Softbound: ISBN 0-87954-404-X / $29.95
Hardbound: ISBN 0-87954-403-1 / $39.95

THE NONPROFIT ENTREPRENEUR: Creating Ventures to Earn Income

Edited by Edward Skloot

In a collection of writings by the nation's top practitioners and advisors in nonprofit enterprise, Edward Skloot demonstrates how nonprofits can launch successful earned-income enterprises without compromising their missions. Topics covered include legal issues, marketing techniques, business planning, avoiding the pitfalls of venturing for smaller nonprofits, and a special section on museums and their retail operations.

September 1988 / ISBN 0-87954-239-X / $19.95

A NONPROFIT ORGANIZATION OPERATING MANUAL: Planning for Survival and Growth

by Arnold J. Olenick and Philip R. Olenick

This desk manual for nonprofit executives covers all aspects of starting and managing a nonprofit. The authors discuss legal problems, obtaining tax exemption, organizational planning and development, and board relations; operational, proposal, cash, and capital budgeting; marketing, grant proposals, fundraising, and for-profit ventures; computerization; and tax planning and compliance.

July 1991 / ISBN 0-87954-293-4 / $29.95

PEOPLE POWER: SERVICE, ADVOCACY, EMPOWERMENT

by Brian O'Connell

People Power, a selection of Brian O'Connell's writings, provides commentary on the nonprofit world. The 25+ essays included in this volume range from analyses of the role of voluntarism in American life, to advice for nonprofit managers, to suggestions for developing and strengthening the nonprofit sector of the future.

October 1994 / ISBN 0-87954-563-1 / $24.95

PROMOTING ISSUES AND IDEAS: A Guide to Public Relations for Nonprofit Organizations, Revised Edition

by M Booth & Associates

This newly revised edition presents strategies to attract the interest of the people you wish to influence and inform. Included are the nuts and bolts of advertising, publicity, speech-making, lobbying, and special events; the use of rapidly evolving communication technologies; and crisis management.

December 1995 / ISBN 0-87954-594-1 / $29.95

RAISE MORE MONEY FOR YOUR NONPROFIT ORGANIZATION: A Guide to Evaluating and Improving Your Fundraising

by Anne L. New

Anne New sets guidelines for a fundraising program that will benefit the incipient as well as the established nonprofit organization. A 20-page bibliography highlights useful research and funding directories.

January 1991 / ISBN 0-87954-388-4 / $14.95

SECURING YOUR ORGANIZATION'S FUTURE: A Complete Guide to Fundraising Strategies

by Michael Seltzer

Beginners get bottom-line facts and easy-to-follow worksheets; veteran fundraisers receive a complete review of the basics plus new money-making

ideas. Seltzer supplements his text with an extensive bibliography of selected readings and resource organizations.
March 1987 / ISBN 0-87954-190-3 / $24.95

SUCCEEDING WITH CONSULTANTS: Self-Assessment for the Changing Nonprofit

by Barbara Kibbe and Fred Setterberg

Succeeding with Consultants provides practical advice for nonprofit executives eager to improve their organization's performance. Written by Barbara Kibbe and Fred Setterberg and supported by the David and Lucile Packard Foundation, this book guides nonprofits through the process of selecting and utilizing consultants to strengthen their organization's operations.
April 1992 / ISBN 0-87954-450-3 / $19.95

THE 21ST CENTURY NONPROFIT

by Paul B. Firstenberg

The 21st Century Nonprofit helps nonprofits become more vital social and cultural forces by encouraging managers to adopt strategies developed by the for-profit sector in recent years, including expanding their revenue base by diversifying grant sources, exploiting the possibilities of for-profit enterprises, developing human resources by learning how to attract and retain talented people, and exploring the nature of leadership through short profiles of three non-profit CEOs.
July 1996 / Softcover / ISBN 0-87954-672-7 / $34.95
Hardcover / ISBN 0-87594-652-2 / $39.95

MEMBERSHIP PROGRAM

ASSOCIATES PROGRAM
Direct Line to Fundraising Information

Annual membership in the Associates Program provides vital information on a timely basis, including information from:

— Foundation and corporate annual reports, brochures, press releases, grants lists, and other announcements

— IRS 990-PF information returns for all 38,800 active grantmaking U.S. foundations—often the only source of information on small foundations

— Electronic databases, books, and periodicals on the grantmaking field, including materials on regulation and nonprofit management

• The Associates Program provides access to this information via a toll-free telephone number. The annual fee of $495 entitles you to ten toll-free telephone reference calls per month. Additional calls can be made at the rate of $30 per ten calls.

- Membership in the Associates Program allows you to request custom searches of the Foundation Center's computerized databases, which contain information on some 40,000 U.S. founda tions and corporate givers. There is an additional charge for this service.

- Associates Program members may request photocopies of key documents. Important information from 990-PFs, annual reports, application guidelines, and other resources can be copied and either mailed or faxed to your office. The fee for this service, available only to Associate Members, is $2.00 for the first page of material and $1.00 for each additional page. Fax service is available at an additional charge.

- All Associates Program members receive the Associates Program quarterly newsletter, which provides news and information about new foundations, changes in boards of directors, new programs, and announcements of publications issued by both the Foundation Center and other publishers in the field.

For more information call 1-800-424-9836.

FOUNDATION CENTER DATABASES

FC Search: The Foundation Center's Database on CD-ROM

The Foundation Center's comprehensive database of grantmakers and their associated grants may now be accessed in a fully searchable CD-ROM format. *FC Search* contains the Center's entire universe of over 43,000 grantmaker records, including active foundations and corporate giving programs in the United States. It also includes nearly 200,000 recent grant awards of the largest foundations and the names of nearly 180,000 trustees, officers, and donors which can be quickly linked to their foundation affiliations.

Grantseekers and other researchers may select multiple criteria and create customized prospect lists which can be printed or saved. Basic or Advanced search modes and special search options enable users to make searches as broad or as specific as required. Up to 21 different criteria may be selected:

- grantmaker name
- grantmaker type
- grantmaker city
- grantmaker state
- geographic focus
- fields of interest
- types of support
- total assets

- total giving
- trustees, officers, and donors
- establishment date
- corporate name
- corporate location
- recipient name
- recipient type

- recipient city
- recipient state
- subject
- grant amount
- year grant authorized
- text search field

FC Search is a sophisticated fundraising research tool, but it is also user-friendly. It has been developed with both the novice and experienced researcher in mind. Assistance is available through Online Help, a *User Manual* that accompanies *FC Search*, as well as through a free user Hotline. A mid-year update disk is included in the purchase price.

Minimum System Requirements:

- IBM-compatible PC
- Microsoft Windows 3.1
- CD-ROM Drive
- 486DX microprocessor
- 8MB memory

FC Search, *1997 edition issued Spring 1997 (prices include Fall 1997 update disk plus one User Manual).*

Standalone (single user) version ($1,195)

Network (2–8 users at a single site) version: $1,495*

Additional copies of User Manual: *$19.95*

*Larger local area network versions and wide area network versions are also available. For more information, call the **FC Search Hotline (Mon–Fri., 9 am–5 pm EST) 1-800-478-4661.**

Foundation and Grants Information Online

The Foundation Center offers two databases on Dialog through Knight-Ridder Information Services. Computer access lets you design your own search for the foundations and corporate givers most likely to support your nonprofit organization. Online retrieval provides vital information on funding sources, philanthropic giving, grant application guidelines, and the financial status of foundations to nonprofit organizations seeking funds, grantmaking institutions, corporate contributors, researchers, journalists, and legislators.

Custom computer searching of our databases performed by Center staff is available for a fee upon request. For information on accessing the Center's databases directly, contact Knight-Ridder at 1-800-334-2564.

DIALOG User Manual and Thesaurus, Revised Edition

To facilitate your foundation and corporate giving research in these databases, the Center now offers a revised edition of its *User Manual and Thesaurus.*

November 1995 / ISBN 0-87954-595-X/ $50

THE FOUNDATION CENTER'S WORLD WIDE WEB SITE (http://fdncenter.org)

The Foundation Center's World Wide Web site (http://fdncenter.org) is an online source of fundraising information. Updated and expanded daily, the Center's site provides grantseekers, grantmakers, researchers, journalists, and the general public with access to a range of valuable resources, among them:

- A searchable Grantmaker Information directory with annotated links to more than 150 individual grantmaker sites.

- *Philanthropy News Digest*, a weekly compendium of philanthropy-related articles abstracted from major print and online media outlets.

- An Electronic Reference Desk, where users can find answers to frequently asked questions, an online librarian to respond to specific questions about grantseeking and the Foundation Center, and annotated links to useful nonprofit and philanthropic information resources.

- A Fundraising Process directory featuring the Proposal Writing Short Course, glossary, tips on the fundraising process, and downloadable common grant application forms.

- A Training and Seminars directory with information about Center-sponsored orientations and training seminars.

- A Libraries and Locations directory, which lists the locations of the Center's 200+ Cooperating Collections nationwide, and covers the activities and resources at our five libraries.

There is a low-bandwidth mirror site (http://fdncenter.org/2index.html) —a resource for visitors with slower modems and Internet connections as well as for those who want to access the information they need as quickly as possible. The Center's publications and CD-ROM may also be ordered via the site's downloadable or interactive order forms.

About the Authors

Jane C. Geever is president of J. C. Geever, Inc., a development consulting firm in New York City founded by Ms. Geever in 1975. The firm is a longstanding member of the American Association of Fund-Raising Counsel (AAFRC).

For 21 years, J. C. Geever, Inc., has been successful in helping nonprofits to obtain funding from foundations, corporations, and individuals.

Ms. Geever is a member of the National Society of Fund Raising Executives (NSFRE) and the Philanthropic Advisory Council for the Better Business Bureau in New York.

Patricia McNeill has been actively involved in fundraising for more than 15 years. As executive vice president of J. C. Geever, Inc., she counseled a wide variety of nonprofit organizations on foundation and corporate fundraising, capital campaigns, board development, and management issues. She is a member of NSFRE and Women in Financial Development.